Praise

When the Sky is Falling

"I love Eric's writing. It is filled with passion and creativity and he calls us all to a firm and authentic faith. This is a great book, one we should all be challenged by and share with others!"

- **Jud Wilhite**, author of *Throw It Down*, senior pastor of Central Christian Church, Las Vegas

If you are in pain, as are tens of millions of your neighbors in this sketchy post 9/11 world, chances are your spiritual vision has narrowed and your hearing has become muffled. Your circumstances may have overwhelmed your faith. Eric Sandras and his family have faced the full brunt of circumstantial breakdown and yet this author has found a spark of faith which he has fanned into full flame in this book. Buy a stack and give it to everyone you know who is hurting.

- **David Housholder**, author of *The Blackberry Bush* and lead teacher at Robinwood Church

Buck Naked Faith

"Finally, someone not only willing to speak up to the church—'The Emperor has no clothes'—but someone offering robes of righteousness to all who come."

- **Leonard Sweet**, author

Plastic Jesus

"In *Plastic Jesus*, I experienced good humor, emotional and relational honesty, and fresh help to move from what Eric calls 'spiritual suburbia' to a new home in Christ. I heartily recommend *Plastic Jesus* to anyone wanting a real Jesus and a real relationship with him."

— **Todd Hunter**, Bishop of the Anglican Church in North America, author of *The Outsider Interviews*

WHEN THE SKY IS FALLING

Finding Faith & Hope in Life's Crises

ERIC SANDRAS, PHD

ampelon publishing
Boise, ID

When the Sky is Falling
Copyright ©2012 by Eric Sandras

ISBN: 978-0-9840095-8-9
Printed in the United States of America

To order other Ampelon Publishing products, visit us on the web at: www.ampelonpublishing.com

Cover design: Damonza.com

Dedication

To Cindy: my wife, my friend, my companion. You have persevered and constantly find a thread of hope to hold onto. Thanks for being by my side.

To those who have yet to struggle or suffer through crisis: May you find some wisdom in the pages of this book and some hope in the God above it.

Acknowledgments

D.C. Jacobson & Associates and Jason Chatraw: You believed in the relevance and message of this book even when often I didn't. Thanks for being a ray of hope.

My friends at Jives Coffee of Manitou Springs, CO: Thanks for serving up great java and comfortable refuge while this broke bloke sat rent free for too many hours.

Elaine Colvin of the Writer's Information Network. Helping aspiring writers is not your career path—it is your calling.

Friends—too many to list here, but too dear to exclude: your words of encouragement, gifts of support, and prayers of concern have carried us more than you will ever know.

Table of Contents

A note from Dr. E: Most books are broken up into neat and orderly sections, balancing the book out like a fine 7-course dinner. Not this one. Because, perhaps like yours, my life these days is just broken up. So the sections below aren't really chapters per say, just pieces. Picked up a bit at a time. I pray, my friend, that those pieces will offer you a ray of hope even if the sky is falling.

Chapter 1

Needing A Ray Of Hope

I found myself in trouble and went looking for my Lord;
my life was an open wound that wouldn't heal.
When friends said, "Everything will turn out all right,"
I didn't believe a word they said.
I remember God—and shake my head.
I bow my head—then wring my hands.
I'm awake all night—not a wink of sleep;
I can't even say what's bothering me.
I go over the days one by one,
I ponder the years gone by.
I strum my lute all through the night,
wondering how to get my life together.
- **unknownperson @Psalm 77:2-6 (MSG)**

Frustration with my life had seemingly reached a peak as I stood staring at my stress-worn face in the mirror. Like a pod of dandelion spores caught up in a hurricane, it seemed everything in my life was getting blown away and no matter what I tried, I just couldn't stop it.

I could feel the light I had so faithfully carried for thirty years being sucked into the vortex of disbelief and disillusionment, like the beginning stages of a cosmic black hole in my soul. Honestly, I felt I was simultaneously about to implode under the crushing weight of no longer being able to support my family and emotionally explode with anger towards those who unknowingly decided to send my life into a tailspin.

Sometimes it's hard to direct anger and frustration back to the source. At this stage any one thing going wrong in my life would have been manageable, but it was the convergence of just too many things that seemed to be conspiring against me that was bringing my marriage, my faith, and me to the breaking point.

"Whose fault was it? Who should I pummel with my frustration and grief?" I muttered so often to myself.

The church board that laid me off?
The bank that was trying to take my home?
The cancer that wanted to invade my body?
Maybe it's God's fault… yeah, God. It must be God's fault.

My reasoning seemed sound. After all, He was supposed to ultimately be in control of the universe, particularly my universe. So what went wrong?

There I was, staring at a disillusioned 45-year-old man who, two short years ago, was working his dream job as a teaching pastor in a large Southern California mega-church and as a part-time professor at a local community college. Now I was packing what personal belongings hadn't sold on Craigslist, making plans to move my family in with my parents, and wondering how we were going to afford college for my daughter, school supplies for my son, and grief therapy for my wife.

The unraveling of my perfect world seemed to have reached a crescendo, but I had reached that crescendo three or four times before and the storm only seemed to intensify. So today, instead of laying claim to my faith, I was embracing failure more as a friend than an enemy.

Honestly, I was giving up. The only ray of hope I had was that I actually had a place to move. Some friends I knew didn't even have that. It was my father who took that little ray of hope and multiplied it that day. As I chatted with him that afternoon the only words I could muster were, "I can't believe this. Here I come—an unemployed, homeless, cancer victim. Are you sure you and mom want that?"

His response chided me a bit, "Actually, only one of those three is true. You may be unemployed, but you do have a home to come to and you are a cancer survivor, not a victim."

Okay, so on those words of wisdom my whole world didn't turn and get pretty like a Cinderella story, but the small ray of hope I had somehow got bigger. And that experience got me thinking. Over the course of my two-year "unraveling," there had been a number of experiences like the one with my dad. Just when I felt the dark thunder clouds of life were about to snuff out the last bit of light I could perceive, someone or something, provided just enough insight or encouragement help me carry on another day.

I understand light always pierces darkness—after all, I'm a preacher. But I have also seen how thunder clouds can cause a dark, damp heaviness that is almost as bad as the night.

Hold on. Let's put on the brakes for a moment...

At this point you're probably asking yourself how this book fits under the self-help/faithful living category. Or you're beginning to wonder if I'm writing the preamble to a country song. I assure you the latter is not true. When you are through reading, I'll let you decide if these pages actually helped your own journey through the valley of the shadows or just reinforced your own disillusionment.

Of course, my prayer is that you'll find yourself in the category of some elite people throughout history—people who refused to see themselves as victims, but found a way to truly become survivors and, in many cases, conquerors. There are those who took the worst of life's circumstances and found a way to use it to bless others and multiply rays of hope someone in else's life. They actually moved from conquering the worst seasons of their lives to becoming more than conquerors in all seasons of their lives.

However, this book isn't intended to be an inspirational history lesson where I tell you other people's stories that I've read about in some soupy book or magazine—stories where we become experts on what we are not experiencing. This book is about *you* and *me*: personal and intense; focused and purposeful. Together, over these pages, I pray we emerge through the storm to the promise of calmer waters on the other side. Let's not pretend the storm doesn't exist, nor placate each other with cheesy Christianese slogans or boardroom motivational posters. Instead, may we purpose to use whatever tool, whatever hope, whatever wisdom we can garner to make it through today. Because I believe if we make it through today, without shipwrecking our faith or our lives, there is a tomorrow.

Think about it this way, whether you are 10 or 110, you still have your whole life ahead of you. Somehow, someway, may we finish well. And finishing well begins with choosing this day to live… No, not just live, but live well … even when life is telling us not to.

Chapter 2

How Nachos Changed My Life

*Keep your guard up. You're not the only ones plunged into these
hard times. It's the same with Christians all over the world. So
keep a firm grip on the faith. The suffering won't last forever.*
- Peter @1Peter 5:9 (MSG)

Not long before the unraveling of my life began, I
was sharing nachos and buffalo wings at a local
restaurant with my friend Sandy. Sandy's a great
guy. Full of artistic creativity and compassion for the poor.
We were hanging out pontificating about the higher things
of theology like pastors do... Actually, I think we are talking
about an old, rusted out VW bus he bought and how he was
trying to resurrect it to call it his own. In the midst of our
conversation, our waitress Kristina, reached across the table
to place our mountainous cheese-laden nachos and steamy
wings in front of us.

What caught my eye was her freshly inked forearm. Two
monstrous orchid flowers climbed up her slender right arm.
One was colored deep purple and the other a bright red.

Flippantly I said, "Wow, you must really like orchids."

"No, not really," came the reply. "But they aren't there
for me. They are there for my mom and sister."

Now my curiosity was aroused, so I pried a bit more, "So your mom likes flowers?"

Kristina's voice softened a bit as she reflected on her forearm décor, "The flowers are for my mom and sister. The purple one is for my sister. She has had brain cancer for 11 years now, and is still fighting it. This red one here is for my mom. Mom has a blood disease that produces too many platelets. When she gets the smallest of cuts, it clots way too fast and still bleeds inside. Every time I see this tattoo it reminds me to pray for them, and of just how strong they are. The tattoo reminds me every day that I am blessed to not have either of these hereditary diseases... Would you like some more ice tea?"

I whimpered a little and responded, "Yes, please," as I fought back a few tears.

Wow, what a heartfelt story. So much pain and hopefulness tatted onto one person's arm. Sandy's and my conversation shifted from rusted VW busses to flowered tattoos.[1]

As we were leaving the restaurant that afternoon, Kristina caught me to say thank you.

Thinking she was thanking me for my generous tip I replied, "Oh that's fine, I took a lot of your time today."

"No, not for the tip, but for listening to my story. You see, we just had a lady in here the other day who left a letter for my manager telling him that when he allows waitresses with tattoos to serve, it makes the whole restaurant seem dirty. I was hurt because, unlike you two, she didn't know my story."

Okay, now I was really touched and wishing I would have left more than 18.5%. Again I whimpered out a, "You're welcome."

The encounter got Sandy and I pondering how many people we have known with similar tattoo stories. It seemed so many people these days were inking themselves not for décor but for memorial. In the bigger context we realized that at some point in this human journey, everyone gets marked with pain or loss.[2] Despite what "Leave it to Beaver" implied and many churches attempt to impose about the perfect life and the perfect family, it just doesn't seem to exist.

Shared pain also means shared humanity. And regardless of whether you use ink on your skin or ink on a pad of paper to express yourself—whether you choose to release balloons or send money to orphans in memorial of pain—we all find a way for pain and grief to leak out. Sometimes those choices lend themselves towards our healing, and other times they detract from it.

The point is that we are all marked by pain, frustration, loss, and disillusionment. Sometimes by choices we make, and sometimes by choices others make towards us. It is when that pain and disillusionment want to snuff out the life you have to share with others that adjustments need to be made. I pray in the following pages you will continue to find hope multiplied and disillusionment subsiding.

Pray this:

Behold me, my beloved Jesus,
weighed down under the burden of my trials and sufferings,
I cast myself at Your feet,
that You may renew my strength and my courage,
while I rest here in Your presence.
Permit me to lay down my cross in Your sacred heart,
for only Your infinite goodness can sustain me;
only Your love can help me bear my cross;
only Your powerful hand can lighten its weight.
O Divine King, Jesus,
whose heart is so compassionate to the afflicted,
I wish to live in You;
suffer and die in You.
During my life be to me my model and my support;
At the hour of my death,
be my hope and my refuge.
Amen.[3]

Ponder This:

We all know people who have been made much meaner and more irritable and more intolerable to live with by suffering: it is not right to say that all suffering perfects. It only perfects one type of person… the one who accepts the call of God in Christ Jesus.

- Oswald Chambers

Simon, I've prayed for you in particular that you not give in or give out. When you have come through the time of testing, turn to your companions and give them a fresh start."

- **Jesus @Luke 22:31 (MSG)**

A poor youngster with some wisdom
is better off than an old but foolish king
who doesn't know which end is up.
I saw a youth just like this start with nothing
and go from rags to riches,
and I saw everyone rally to the rule
of this young successor to the king.
Even so, the excitement died quickly,
the throngs of people soon lost interest.
Can't you see it's only smoke? And spitting into the wind?
King Solomon @Ecclesiastes 4:13-16 (MSG)

Believe This:

I refuse to believe I am alone in my crisis. Though my circumstances may be unique, my discontentment and disillusionment are not. There are others who have shared or are currently sharing my struggles. Some of them have overcome, some have not. Today I will choose to try to overcome. I will not let my pain turn to isolation.

Chapter 3

When God Doesn't Show Up

Listen, God! Please, pay attention!
Can you make sense of these ramblings, my groans and cries?
King-God, I need your help.
Every morning you'll hear me at it again.
Every morning I lay out the pieces of my life
on your altar and watch for fire to descend.
—David @Psalm 5:1-3 (MSG)

The crowd waiting outside the University of Southern California's (USC) Galen Center surprised even me—a veteran church conference junkie. Thousands of people lined up in 85-degree weather, waiting well over two hours just to get prime seats during this general admission faith healing, kingdom building, charismatic preaching extravaganza.

The speaker was one of the hottest new faith preachers on the circuit and was setting the East Coast ablaze with his claims of healing, revival and preaching. Since so many of my peers were "into it" I thought I would go and experience firsthand what all the hype was about. Besides, I never shy away from a free dose of God's empowering presence.

I grabbed an aisle seat about 25 rows up from left corner

of the stage. It provided a great view and easy escape route without having to climb past twenty others in my row who would be waving arms and dancing frantically. As I sat, I asked God to settle down my critical heart and allow me to just be present. Something I should do even as I write this chapter…

Directly in front of me sat five of the coolest-looking urban young people I normally would only see in a Forever21 or Abercrombie catalog. They had rad body piercings, not the overdone pin-cushion look; old-looking, faded jeans with just the right amount of worn spots (though they probably paid $100 for them); and just the right amount of tattoo color. I was slightly jealous.

But what really caught my eye was the five- or six-year-old child one of the couples held. His skin was pale, eyes sunken and dark, and he was almost bone thin. I had seen such conditions before and, clearly, their poor son was being ravaged by Leukemia. They held him tight, and the hip, urban couple's friends continuously cycled around him, patting him on the head and whispering comfort into his ears. I knew they were there for a miracle, and my heart wanted the same for them.

Just to my left across the aisle was a couple who couldn't appear more different. They were Chinese in appearance, dressed to the hilt like couples one would expect to see on a Sunday morning at one of those suburban comfort churches where wealth and status try to supersede transparency and humility. But they obviously shared a common hope with my hipster urban friends.

Sitting with them was a boy no older than ten who was in constant motion, clearly agitated by all the people and commotion, yet unable or unwilling to make eye contact with his father when talked to. Not until mom finally pulled out a PSP (hand-held game device for you non-gamers) from her purse did he settle down and focus. My across-the-aisle diagnosis: moderate autism. My heart began to hope for their miracle as well.

Worship was intense and powerful. Nine thousand-plus people focused on God and His presence could raise the roof off of most any gathering. The roving cameras and flashing lights reminded me of being at a U2 concert. The synergy in the room was tangible. My faith was growing, and my expectation of God healing these two boys was also growing.

As worship drew to a close there was a series of welcomes to honored guests, pastors, and important people. Then the main guy came on stage. He was rough around the edges and preached with a frenzy. He talked about money, giving to his movement so it could move to L.A. and reach millions of souls, and told stories of lots of miracles that had been happening in other places. The word charismatic doesn't do him justice. He whipped the crowd into a faith frenzy quicker than a Chihuahua on RedBull.

Then came the time for healings. I could see the hope and excitement in both couples as they left their seats and made their way down the aisle towards the stage area. I'm not sure if my urban friends had a religious bone in their bodies prior to this event, but they had hope… they had faith… they had desperation for God to do something. As I've read the Bible, isn't that often enough?

As they got to the floor level each couple was greeted by some bouncer-looking guys. They seemed to be interviewed in some fashion because they talked for a minute and then seemed to introduce the bouncer dudes to their children.

The Chinese boy was pretty fidgety by this point and with a somewhat tender but firm gesture Mr. Bouncer Guy motioned them back up the aisle. As the father turned, I saw more embarrassment and shame on his face than anger or disappointment. They humbly returned to their seats, and Mom gave their son the PSP again. They would have to hold out for the general prayer and not have access to the prayer team in person.

My urban friends persevered a bit longer. Their bouncer listened intently, looked at his pad of paper a few times, and looked down repeatedly, shaking his head no. The hipster friends in front of me kept standing on their tippy-toes to get a better view and try to interpret what was going on. Then it happened…

They turned around and faced the long walk back up those steps of rejection. Mom was in tears as she held her boy. Dad simply looked shocked and numb. They returned to their friends who immediately wrapped arms around them and gave them more support and love than many church homegroups I've seen. Then silently, while the frenzy continued onstage, they all turned and walked toward the exit.

I couldn't help but begin to cry. The pastor in me

wanted to comfort them, the evangelist in me wanted to be God's lawyer for Him, and the father in me just wanted to cry with them. I was paralyzed and frozen for a few minutes. Finally, I couldn't stand it any longer and I ran up the steps to find my urban friends. I wanted to do something… anything to help them process this disappointment.

I quickly moved from exit point to exit point looking for my disillusioned yet fashionable friends, but to no avail. I was too late. They were gone, set adrift into the land of disillusionment.

I returned to my seat and sat through most of the rest of the event. My Chinese friends tried patiently to wait it out. Twice they had stood for prayers of blessing and anointing. At one point their hopes peaked as the speaker was rattling off a list of what must have been thirty or forty illnesses that God wanted to heal… oddly autism didn't make the list. Still, they stood faithfully and devoutly garnering any blessing that may drift their way, but after another 45 minutes their son had reached his limit. So while another offering was being taken, they took their boy in hand and exited. We made eye contact, and all I could do was muster a compassionate smile and gesture that I would be praying for them. He humbly nodded and whispered thank you.

Now I'm nervous. As people read this passage I see one of two things happening, neither of which is my intention. There are those who are offended that I would write anything that would appear to undermine such faith healing gatherings and/or such "men/women of God." I can see the Twitter-Bombs stacking up accusing me of negating all the good that such events bring or my undermining the actual miracles that may occur.

And on the other side, I'm afraid I may be steering people away from actually pursuing a miracle in their life. After reading my experience at this one event, I'm afraid I may have just given someone such a healthy dose of skepticism that they now see all faith preachers on the same plain as a snake charmer or 1-900-psychic.

Honestly, neither is my intention. Maybe because I've been around awhile, but I don't fall into the "either/or" mentality of faith. The kind that says either this is all God or none God. Often it seems to be a mix of the two. People bring their own faith to such events—their own belief systems—and even preachers, whether they admit it or not, are seldom pure in their theology or motives.

I've had the privilege of praying for the sick and watching as hearing is restored, or the crippled walk, or cancer recedes. As well, I've seen God work through charlatans and manipulators—bringing amazing answers to prayers to people's lives, whether by holding their hand to the television screen or being touched by the "anointed one" themselves.

So becoming the judge and jury of such events and people is not my role. Instead, I want to focus on the "now what?" of such experiences. What happens when God doesn't show up? At least in the way we expected or really, really, desperately wanted Him to.

Faith in a higher power can sure feel like a roller coaster.

At times, we sense and feel strong elation and belief. Then other times, we wonder where God is and feel like we are crying out in the dark. I know theologically God is always there, but why doesn't my heart believe it sometimes? Why do my experiences so often seem to say otherwise? Sometimes it is a matter of perspective.

Pray this:

I arise today
Through the strength of Christ's birth and His baptism,
Through the strength of His crucifixion and His burial,
Through the strength of His resurrection and His ascension,
Through the strength of His descent for the judgment of doom.
I arise today
Through the strength of the love of cherubim,
In obedience of angels,
In service of archangels,
In the hope of resurrection to meet with reward,
In the prayers of patriarchs,
In preachings of the apostles,
In faiths of confessors,
In innocence of virgins,
In deeds of righteous men.
I arise today through the strength of Heaven
the rays of the sun,
the radiance of the moon,
the splendor of fire,
the speed of lightning,
the swiftness of the wind,
the depth of the sea,
the stability of the earth
the firmness of rock.
I arise today through the power of God:
God's might to comfort me,

God's wisdom to guide me,
God's eye to look before me,
God's ear to hear me,
God's word to speak for me,
God's hand to lead me,
God's way to lie before me,
God's shield to protect me,
God's Heavenly Host to save me
from the snares of the devil,
from temptations to sin,
from all who wish me ill,
from near and afar,
alone and with others.
May Christ shield me today
against poison and fire,
against drowning and wounding,
so that I may fulfill my mission
and bear fruit in abundance.
Christ behind and before me,
Christ beneath and above me,
Christ with me and in me,
Christ around and about me,
Christ on my right and on my left,
Christ when I lie down at night,
Christ when I rise in the morning,
Christ in the heart of every man who thinks of me,
Christ in the mouth of everyone that speaks of me,
Christ in every eye that sees me,
Christ in every ear that hears me.
I arise today
Through a mighty strength, the invocation of the Trinity,
Through a belief in the Threeness, Through confession of the
Oneness
Of the Creator of creation.

— **The Lorica of St. Patrick**[4]

Ponder This:

"I thank the Lord that, even though things were so wrong in my life here, I finally was brought to the realization of what all those struggles were about. There are some wonderful things from your painful past, things with a beauty you may not have realized at the time."

- **Ravi Zacharias**, from his book
Walking from East to West: God in the Shadows

Lord, I have heard the news about you;
I am amazed at what you have done.
Lord, do great things once again in our time;
make those things happen again in our own days.
Even when you are angry,
remember to be kind.
- **The Prophet @Habakkuk 3:2 (NCV)**

Believe This:

The hardest choice I make today is to trust a God who does not make sense. To trust in a God who is Love though I may not feel love at that moment. Trust is not expecting things to go the way I want—trust is believing somehow, someway, God will carry me through even the most desperate of circumstances.

Chapter 4

When God Abandoned Me
for a Brazilian Mother

You, God—don't put off my rescue!
Hurry and help me!
Don't let them cut my throat;
don't let those mongrels devour me.
If you don't show up soon,
I'm done for...
David @Psalm 22:19-21 (MSG)

In one of my previous books, *Plastic Jesus*, I shared a
story of disillusionment that came out of my time in
Brazil. My team and I were ministering in the small river
village of Porto de Moz. We'd been there for a week. I had
a good friend who was the pastor of a small church in this
rural, impoverished community, which is only accessible by
boat or plane.

Our presence as American missionaries provided some
great publicity for the final evening's church meeting. A hun-
dred or so people packed the minuscule structure, and God
was on the move. I preached what I thought was a powerful
word for the community, and the air was charged with faith
and encouragement. I can't recall ever feeling so much in
"the zone."

Then it happened. The mass of people up front parted like the Red Sea and sheepishly walking toward me was a mother with her six-year-old boy tucked behind her. I could tell by the reaction of those around that this young woman was well-known. Through the translator, she simply said, "Please ask that God would heal my son." She showed me the boy, who was paralyzed down the entire left side of his body. Half his face drooped. His left arm and leg hung limp and lifeless.

As I knelt down to be eye-to-eye with this precious child, he moved to hide behind his mother's hip. His life had been six years of hell. In a land where survival is the goal and weakness is a liability, he had been teased, beaten, and ridiculed. But a mother's love had brought him to a place of worship that night.

I reached out my hand and took hold of his good one. Immediately something began to surge through me like liquid love. It's hard to explain, but I loved this boy as my own. He felt it also, because he immediately stepped away from his mother and moved toward me. I looked into his hallow, but trusting eyes, and began to pray for his physical healing.

Oh, my faith was so high at that point. Still feeling the presence of God from the meeting, coupled with the love and compassion I had for this young man, I knew God would heal this boy. And so I prayed. I could still feel the waves of liquid love flowing through me, but there was no physical manifestation of healing occurring in his body.

My faith thermometer dipped just a bit.

While I prayed more holy words out loud, I found myself silently beginning to negotiate with God.

Lord, all these people are here and experiencing Your presence. What a statement it will make to this community when You heal this boy.

Nothing…

Jesus, this is going to be a really bad P.R. move if this boy doesn't leave here healed. I know how much You love him; now please heal him.

Still nothing…

Negotiation was turning to begging, while I tried to keep up my very best faith-filled persona.

Jesus, I've done what You've asked me to do on this trip. I've left my family at home and spent all this time and money to be here. Please, at least for me, would You heal this child!

I began to feel an unholy vacuum within.

Jesus, this is just not right. This mother comes to You as her only hope and You are going to let her leave here shattered. That's just not right.

At that point, the negotiating ceased. I knew the healing wasn't going to happen, though I didn't know why. I stood up and let go of the little boy's hand. In my heart, all of the incredible things God had been doing that night were being crushed under the weight of my burgeoning disillusionment and embarrassment.

I gave my best cheesy Christian pastoral smile to the mother and turned to walk away. I wanted to run and hide, but my heart made me turn and say one last thing to the mom.

"Look, I don't know why God didn't heal your son. I wish I did. But I can tell you one thing, He loves your boy. I have never felt so much love and mercy flowing through me from God toward an individual as when I touched his hand. I'm sorry."

As I turned to leave, the mother burst into tears.

"God loves my son! God loves my son!" she kept saying.

As I found out later, when she had been eight months pregnant, her brother and another guy got into an argument and her brother was murdered right in front of her. The horror of that trauma apparently sent her into premature labor. That crisis coupled with poor medical procedures and facilities seemed to have influenced the brain damage that caused the paralysis her son had lived with ever since.

She had thought God had abandoned them both. Perhaps more than healing of the body, they both needed healing of the heart and Jesus met them at that place.

I struggled for a long time wondering why God wouldn't answer my prayers of physical healing for that boy. Then one day I realized that maybe I would never hear from God about that situation, that I may never know why He didn't work in the way I thought best, and that God was asking me to choose to be okay with that. I understood that I had to choose to trust Him, and not allow discouragement to cause me to stop praying for the sick or caring for the broken.

But how would I be able to choose trust in the midst of doubt and disillusionment? I can't tell you this realization came through some amazing revelation off watching a tele-vangelist. I can't tell you I received a FedEx package from the Vatican containing a book entitled *"Answers to Faith's Hardest Questions."*

Nope. Restored faith came through wrestling with God in the silence. It came through re-evaluating many of my preconceived ideas regarding how God should work on my behalf. It came through remembering all the times in my journey when I had seen God act in me and through me. As a result, I was not willing to let the acid of disillusionment eat up my faith. God's love and forgiveness in my own life had just been too powerful and too redemptive to let something like this destroy my love for Him.

So I chose to trust and let God's way be a mystery and not a misery in my life—and then God spoke, "Eric, if you want the thrill of victory, you will have to learn to live with the agony of defeat. I am more concerned with your trust in me than I am your understanding of me."

And that's my point. I could spend countless theological hours till I'm blue in the *faith* trying to figure out why God seems to show up in some circumstances and not in others. Why sometimes I pray for a front row parking spot and – BOOM – there it is, while at the same moment, someone with a real need has no answer.

But do I still trust?

Do I choose to believe that maybe, just maybe, there is a bigger story going on besides just mine?

So where was God when my hip urban friends pulled away in what I assume was a pimped out Nissan Cube or plush Land Rover? He was in the backseat—crying. He was crying with them as hope seemed to be seeping out of their lives like a punctured tire.

Cancer was never God's intention, nor is it His invention, but being present in the midst of such fear and heartache is His specialty.

Where was he when such faithful perseverance turned to dust with my Chinese friends? He was right there with them as they opened the Bible again to help them make sense out of life when life doesn't make sense. He was in the room with their boy, as he always is.

Autism was never His intention for humanity, but being present in the midst of the frustration is His specialty.

I think we all can find God's presence, even when He doesn't show up on stage, or the numbers on a lottery ticket, or even at church prayer meetings. He's there in our disillusionment and pain, just like He has always been.

Of course that doesn't guarantee that things will get better before they get worse…

Pray this:

An I Don't Know Prayer[5]

Sometimes, Heavenly Father
The answer has to be 'I don't know'
'I don't know why
there is so much suffering in the world'
'I don't know why
that child was not restored to full health'
'I don't know why
people can be so cruel, uncaring, selfish'
Platitudes cannot console a grieving parent,
a starving child,
a battered wife.
Sometimes, Heavenly Father
our faith is challenged by this world,
a world that is less concerned with others
than with self.
Sometimes, in being honest,
we open ourselves to ridicule.
The world would prefer certainty,
but the only certainty is You,
who created humankind with the capacity
for good and ill,
and gave the world Your Son,
whom we crucified.
'I don't know'
might seem a lame excuse to some,
uncertainty,
but we trust in Your eternal love
for a mankind which has fallen.
We thank You that we are not robots
but have freedom of choice.
Help us to make right choices,
choices that affect lives.

Help us to play our part in changing this world,
rather than merely sitting back as spectators
and criticizing.
Help us to see this world
through your eyes of love

Ponder this:

Most of the verses written about praise in God's Word were voiced by people faced with crushing heartaches, injustice, treachery, slander, and scores of other difficult situations.

– Joni Erickson Tada[6]

Everything can be taken from a man or a woman but one thing: the last of human freedoms to choose one's attitude in any given set of circumstances, to choose one's own way.

- Viktor E. Frankl[7]

Believe this:

My prayers, my hopes, my desires may not be answered in the way I expected—nonetheless, I choose today to believe there is a bigger picture that I do not see. I choose, today, to believe God will somehow find a way to redeem what has caused so much hurt and pain in my life. It may not be today, but it will come. It must come.

Chapter 5

The Unraveling Begins

> Here's a piece of bad luck I've seen happen:
> A man hoards far more wealth than is good for him
> And then loses it all in a bad business deal.
> He fathered a child but hasn't a cent left to give him.
> He arrived naked from the womb of his mother;
> He'll leave in the same condition—with nothing.
> This is bad luck, for sure—naked he came, naked he went.
> So what was the point of working for a salary of smoke?
> All for a miserable life spent in the dark?
> **- King Solomon @Ecclesiastes 5:13-17 (MSG)**

Click…Click…Click… You know that feeling as a roller coaster is climbing its initial ascent?

Click… Click… Click…

You can feel the tension building as the weight of the coaster seems to pull you backwards, yet some powerful force continues to force the contraption you are shackled into higher and higher… and higher…

Click… Click… Click…

As the coaster reaches its crescendo there is this moment of pure excitement, fear, apprehension, and stillness all smooshed together in a high voltage sense of adrenaline.

Click… Click… Whooosh…

There is no turning back. Whether you want on that ride or not is now irrelevant. Whether you survive or wind up a plot scene for a gory horror movie has yet to be known.

I remember riding a coaster at Six Flags in Texas a few years ago with a national board member of one of the largest church movements in the United States. As we approached the launching point at the top of what felt like a bazillion-foot high peak, he leaned over and told me, "Eric, I hope whatever you hear come out of my mouth during the next 45 seconds isn't held against me for the duration of your visit…"

Whoosh…

I'm glad he warned me—though I hardly heard his not-made-for-Sunday-morning verbiage over my girlish screaming.

I remember that same sense of apprehension and excitement as my wife and I were preparing to leave our comfortable, deeply-rooted life in Port Angeles, Washington in order to move to Southern California to go on staff with one of the largest churches in Los Angeles County.

Through much time and prayer, we had decided that even at this point in our lives we would rather take a risk and be wrong than stay comfortable and always wonder if we missed an opportunity. Most of our stuff was pretty worn out or just didn't seem worth the effort to move, so the inventory clearance and garage sales began. In some ways it was quite liberating knowing that my 1980's Member's Only jacket was going to go to some lucky guy or my wife's Barry Manilow 8-track collection was finally going to get some play time in someone else's home.

The experience reminded me of our dear friends, Alan and Julie, who had moved away some years prior. Because they chose to move to a third world country on the other side of the planet, they sold everything—and I mean everything. Mom, Dad, and each of their two sons got to keep one large plastic tub of belongings, plus one "family" tub. I recall descending on their home like a well-meaning vulture looking for bargains and the cool stuff they were giving away. As their departure date approached, their home became more and more vacuous.

Finally, on their last day, all that was left was five plastic tubs sitting in an empty garage. What really caught my attention was the total peace that resided over Alan and Julie. It was then that she made a statement that rocked my consumeristic soul, "You know, it's quite liberating when you realize that it was all really just stuff."

Just a few short years later, Cindy and I were doing a similar thing. Selling most of what we owned and donating the rest, we squeezed the remainder of our belongings into a 6 x 8-foot cargo trailer, said goodbye to the community we had grown to love, and headed off to the next adventure—*Whoosh*…

It wasn't a decision we had made lightly. We had two kids to consider, a house to sell, and a church to release. The timing seemed right, and the pieces came together perfectly.

Our daughter was just about to begin high school, we had a minimum five-year commitment from the church we were joining (that would allow my kids to finish school in one place), and we were debt free. Not that we had much, but our truck and my bumble bee yellow motorcycle were paid for, credit cards were at zero balance, and my kids had been accepted into a great private school, one free of the typical Los Angeles gang/drug influences. So we strapped in, held on, and *Whoosh…*

Arriving in Southern California in June 2006 at the peak of the housing market was a challenge. With rental prices as high as mortgage payments we decided to purchase a home right away. Thankfully, my wife was a business major and has a strict fiscal personality. Me on the other hand, oh mighty man of faith that I was, wanted it all—the pool, the view, the great neighborhood, and the yard with an avocado tree. She, on the other hand, felt that though our lender was able to finagle such a pricey loan, we'd be better off living within our budget. So we purchased just a home. Nothing fancy by any means especially by Southern California standards, but it was just within our budget. At least it had a plum tree. We were stretched a bit, but not over our heads. *Whoosh….*

What began to catch us off guard was how expensive in general Southern California was. Car insurance, food costs, and gas was much higher than our little town of Port Angeles had ever been. School activities and amenities continued to demand our discretionary income. Still with my new dream job at the church, and my wife working administration in the same office, we tightened our belts and made ends meet. *Whoosh…*

Within six months of starting my new job and the purchase of our new home, the economic tsunami of 2006 began to overtake California. By the end of our first year, our home was upside down by $30,000 and it just kept sliding.

Whoosh… Oh, #&~!*

- **January 2008:** Three staff were laid off at the church, and I received a five percent pay cut. I told the executive leaders I had another job opportunity if that would help prevent layoffs, but was promptly informed my position was too vital to allow my departure.

- **February 2008:** In an attempt to modify our loan we were informed by the mortgage company that unless we started missing payments they would not be able to help us. So we sacrificed a near perfect credit score to remain faithful to our loan.

- **March 2008:** Through a meager modification assessment the bank informed us they had made a mistake on the initial tax value of the neighborhood—our payment went up $500/month.

- **April 2008:** My wife had to quit working at the church in order to pursue a job with more hours. This was the first time since we'd been married we weren't serving together.

• **September 2008:** After countless hours and letters to no avail to the mortgage company, we decided to put our home up for short sale.

• **February 2009:** I was informed by the church board and executive leadership that a teaching and recovery ministry pastor was "a luxury the church just couldn't afford anymore," so I was laid off.

That's just six simple bullet points, or 13 measly months, depending how you read it. What fills the gaps between those lines is enough pressure and frustration to blow a NASCAR quality gasket 10 times over. I was on a ride that I just couldn't get off, though I could sense it wasn't going to finish well.

Why did I come here in the first place, leaving such a stable and secure church family?

Why didn't I take the two offers I had last year and jump ship when I could have instead of believing my position was secure?

Why didn't I just pay the extra for rent somewhere instead of feeling the pressure to buy?

Why did God let me get in so far over my head?

Why don't the banks focus on me for just a day or two instead of losing my paperwork for the 4th time?

Why me?

When things are going poorly in life, when frustrations or pain begin to pile up on your life like a bunch of school bullies and you're the nerd, that's when the "Why?'s" begin to flow.

If you've been there trying to stop something that only seems to be building negative momentum, I know you can relate. Between my wife and I, I'm sure we amassed enough "why?'s" to get a top Google ranking. Really, for most of us it isn't the "why?'s" that causes the most heartache, it's the silence after we ask the question.

Just a few weeks back I was having one of my moaning sessions with God (in more spiritual terms, I was lamenting to the Lord…). Here I was, two years later and I was still trying to pick up the pieces of the train wreck my life had become. Still trying to get full-time work, still trying to re-build my credit. Still trying to not let bitterness settle into my heart…

I cried out, "God, this is so unfair. After all Cindy and I have done for You, sacrificed for You, and given to You, this is what I get?"

The response landed on my heart like a ton of theological bricks, "What if I rephrased the question back to you? Eric, after all I've done for you, sacrificed for you, and given you… this is what I get?"

I realized that just asking "why me" was really the selfish way out. Really bringing understanding to tough circumstances means a willingness to ask more thoughtful questions. Try asking:

- Why not me?

- Where does my sense of anger stem from, and where should it most appropriately be directed?

- Am I willing to recognize and accept my responsibility in this equation?

- What do my feelings say about my belief in God, myself, and what life "owes" me?

- Am I willing to accept things I cannot change and adjust to things I can?

- Do I understand I may not be responsible for what happens to me, but I am responsible for my actions in response to what happens to me?

- What have my responses said about me, my character, and my faith? Can I change?

- Am I willing to let some things remain a mystery or accept I may never know the answer to "why"?

Trying to make sense out of senseless occurrences is a lot like trying to teach my dog a card trick. No matter how much mental and emotional energy I put into it, ultimately my pug will just look at me wondering if she is going to get a treat.

But I'm not a dog and our losses were no trick. Over and over in my town I could see what was happening. I would sit in coffee shops and hear people talking over their indulgent foo-foo drinks about how, "They would never walk away from their home responsibilities."

Then some months later, as the economy continued to slide and banks begged for bailouts, they would bemoan over the same foam, "Why did this happen to me?"

Now, I know there are those who could have stayed in their homes and made good on their commitments, but chose to take advantage of an already deteriorating situation. And there are those who got in way over their heads in the buying frenzy of the new millennium and wished they hadn't. Regardless of the personal story, what became evident was that thousands—no, millions—of homeowners in the United States found themselves sucked into the vortex of financial collapse.

But this isn't a chapter about banks, mortgages, and foreclosures. It's about what happens inside of us when things are involuntarily pulled from us instead of generously given to us.

You see, in the past few years I've left home ownership twice. Once voluntarily in pursuit of what I wanted, and once involuntarily because I was just trying to survive. Though the outcome was similar—I sold a bunch of stuff and moved out—what it did to my soul was very different.

A few weeks ago I was playing Monopoly with my family. We are a pretty competitive bunch so the land grabbing, wealth building, take-no-prisoners nature of the game suits us well. Normally I'm on the losing end of such high stakes encounters, but this day was different. The atmosphere around the room was ripe with expectation and greed. I knew this was my day…

Earlier today I won two dollars on my lottery ticket. How could I lose?

Oh, I love the smell of Monopoly money in the evening! The dice were cast, lots were chosen, and I began my day of dominance. First came the railroads, then the strategic purchase of properties to thwart my opponents. I scored all the Orange and began to build my empire. Twelve little houses soon blossomed into towering hotels. Then came my first victim… Bam! Bankrupt and ashamed, my daughter turned over her deeds to my empire and exited the game.

A few more houses on my newly acquired real estate then… Bam! Opponent number two fell to the wayside. With the compassion of a slumlord, I took the remnant of my son's cash and property and excused him from the table. All that was left was my wife and I. All those years of her beating me in Monopoly was about to be rectified with my cunning strategy and dice rolling skills. Refusing to trade with her, she was at my mercy. Within a few short turns it was over… I had conquered all. After sitting back to admire my empire for a few moments, I leaned forward to put the game away. It was then I realized I was sitting by myself.

"Hey, who's gonna help me put all this stuff away?"

With a look only a wife can give a husband, Cindy

looked at me and without a word said, "You earned it. You put it away."

And so with the game over, I put the stuff in a box, put the box in the closet, and sheepishly went to be with my family.

That's it. I put the stuff in a box and went to be with my family. Stuff... box... family... all that effort to amass some stuff and when it was all done, it really didn't matter as much as being with my family did.

That's the point: it really is just stuff. Maybe, like me, you have spent much energy and time trying to get stuff, and having to let it go almost seems unfair. So we spend too much energy holding onto things that someday will be put away and not enough energy holding onto things that can't be forgotten.

The greatest things in life aren't things...

Cindy had that phrase posted in our hallway, surrounded by family pictures as we found ourselves sinking further into financial loss. A constant reminder that some things we have remain priceless even when we are bankrupt.

I'm not here to minimize the heartache and stress associated with losing stuff, but perhaps it doesn't have to be as bad as we think. After all, it is more tragic to lose one's integrity in crisis than one's car.

Realizing the point in my life when I freely gave things away felt liberating, while the point in my life when things were being taken from me felt so violating, was revolutionary. Ironically, the outcome was the same—I just had less stuff. But for a man, a man who wants to be the provider and protector of his family, this was a tough pill to swallow.

Few of us choose loss, because gain feels so much better. Few of us choose to lighten our material load, because amassing treasure has so much more status. Few of us voluntarily give our best away, because giving from our leftovers seems so much more efficient. But there is something to be learned from letting go of stuff—something that can't be learned from holding onto the same.

We begin to learn that stuff doesn't have to define our self-worth or our value. We begin to realize that stuff often attempts to be a surrogate to relationship and meaningful faith. We begin to see that stuff often interferes with substance in our lives. And it is this interference that perversely causes us to hold relationships that matter loosely in order to grasp firm possessions that will be packed away someday anyway.

Now I'm not saying go and sell all your possessions and give them to the poor (though that sounds strangely Biblical). I am saying we must learn to hold our possessions openly and not let our possessions hold us hostage. I am not saying to be passive about the stewardship of your money, nor shirk commitments you have made.

Instead, I invite you to consider the idea that financial freedom isn't the ability to have whatever you want, but the means to have what you need or perhaps to even live beneath your means and share the rest with those who find themselves below that.

Sometimes we must just choose—choose to look at stuff as simply material fodder that can buoy life and look at people as priceless possessions that give life.

However, for many of us it is not the loss of possessions that steals our hope; it is the loss of priceless people in our lives that does the most damage…

Grieving the loss of a loved one is much different than the loss of a credit card...

Pray this:

Heavenly Father, if I should suffer need, and go unclothed, and be in poverty, make my heart prize Thy love, know it, be constrained by it, though I be denied all blessings. It is Thy mercy to afflict and try me with wants, for by these trials I see my sins, and desire severance from them. Let me willingly accept misery, sorrows, temptations, if I can thereby feel sin as the greatest evil, and be delivered from it with gratitude to Thee, acknowledging this as the highest testimony of Thy love.

– **Part of a Puritan Prayer for Contentment**

Ponder this:

You may never know that Jesus is all you need, until Jesus is all you have.

— **Corrie ten Boom**[8]

The way of trust is a movement into obscurity, into the undefined, into ambiguity, not into some predetermined, clearly delineated plan for the future. The next step discloses itself only out of a discernment of God acting in the desert of the present moment. The reality of naked trust is the life of the pilgrim who leaves what is nailed down, obvious, and secure, and walks into the unknown without any rational explanation to justify the decision or guarantee the future. Why? Because God has signaled the movement and offered it his presence and his promise.

— **Brennan Manning**, from his book
Ruthless Trust: The Ragamuffin's Path to God

Believe this:

Stuff is just stuff. I may struggle with the meaning I attach to certain things, but in the struggle I will separate what memory is to be cherished and what thing is to be released.

I choose to let go of the things that I'm an unable to hold onto. Whether lost in a fire, taken through force, or voluntarily given, I will not let my personal worth be determined by what I have or don't have. I am more than the sum of my possessions or the comparison I feel from others.

Chapter 6

Defining Moments
vs.
Refining Moments

"Why bother even trying to do anything with you
when you just keep to your bullheaded ways?
You keep beating your heads against brick walls.
Everything within you protests against you.
From the bottom of your feet to the top of your head,
nothing's working right."
Isaiah @Isaiah 1:5-6 (MSG)

Some poker playing monk once said, "You must play the hand you are dealt."[9] That's easy to do when you are sitting on a royal flush or some other winning set of cards. But when we feel cheated by the cards we are given it gets pretty tempting to cheat back—find some other way, any way to win. Sometimes the allure of feeling good for a moment seems to outweigh the risk of getting caught or making a mistake.

We all have defining moments in our lives. Singular points of time that can yield singular points of failure or singular points of success. Moments where the choice we make will determine the hardship or resilience we will encounter for many weeks or years to come.

Sitting in the famed MGM Grand Hotel poker room that night was going to be just one of those nights for me. The temptation slid across the green felt, not in the form of a handful of poker chips, but in the shroud of an invitation... But let's back up a moment.

Just a few weeks into my move to Las Vegas, the numbness and shock of the past few months began to wear off. It was now May 2009, and my heart and mind began to crumble. Every time I slowed down, my mind sped up. Like a ping-pong ball on steroids, my thoughts bounced back and forth at a frantic pace. The loss of the house, the seeming end of a 15-year career in ministry, and worry regarding Cindy's recuperation from the previous month's major surgery constantly collided with the fear of whether I was going to make money in my new sales job, could I "trust" myself in Vegas without any accountability, and thoughts about the two months that lay ahead of me without Cindy and Carter.

The longest I'd ever been separated from my family was a 20-day missions trip to South America. Now I was staring at six more weeks till they would be able to join me. Thankfully I was able to rent a temporary room from a Christian brother, but isolation did not welcome me as a friend—instead it kept gnawing at my resolve like a herd of termites feasting on a balsa wood shell.

In order to fill time, I played a little poker here and there at various Vegas casinos. Sometimes I could spend three or four hours and make 30 bucks. Other times I would waste three or four hours and spend 30 bucks. Regardless, it slowed the perpetual ping-pong ball bouncing around in my mind.

This night was different. The longer I played, the harder I had to work to squelch noises in my head. Perhaps the pain of disillusionment and loneliness was beginning to scream louder than the voice of reason and commitment that had always had the preferred place in my soul.

To my left I had a wanna-be Harley tough guy from Tuscaloosa. On my right was a petite Asian lady for whom only the waft of her perfume outweighed the bling of her jewelry. And across the table sat a highly inebriated English bloke finishing up a holiday break who couldn't understand how I kept "reading his mind" and taking his money.

The cards flopped, the chips bounced, and the conversations bantered about for a few hours. Whenever the topic drifted to my reason for being "lucky enough" to live in Vegas, I put on my poker face, deflected the question, and prayed the emotional eruption in my soul wasn't leaking out onto the table.

I can't say I'm a pastor… because I'm not anymore. Besides that would be awkward to admit at this table. What am I anyway?

Sure at this point, the standard, "I'm a follower of Christ" or "I'm a good church going man" should have been the immediate response in my head.

But the first thought I had was, "*I'm displaced. Like a man with no country.*"

King, Jack, Ten… what a nice flop to go with my pocket Ace and Queen (that's a straight).

Focus on what's in front of you, Eric…

I bet enough to keep others in, but not give away such a beautiful hand. The Asian lady, who smelled like an air freshener gone berserk, looked at me, squinted as if she was psychic, and then folded. A few others stayed, including my English friend, who apparently was excited because he said something about going out with a bang.

A couple more cards on the table, a couple more bets, and my hand was solid. All that was left was the Englishman and me.

Maybe this is what I should do with my life. Play poker, enjoy a new life, and just live for myself. After all my years giving to others, I deserve a little respite…

To this day I'm not sure if that voice came from within my wounded self or from the outside, so easily penetrating my termite eroded boundaries and morals. All I know is at that moment it made sense. But defining moments are like that. In the moment, either option has as much pull… as much attractiveness as the other. If the decision were easy it wouldn't really be a defining moment, it would be at best a refining moment.

"I'm all in," I said as I pushed my stack to the center of the table. "Me too and God Save the Queen!" came the immediate response.

On most any other hand, his pocket Kings would have

smothered the other player's hand. But his excitement turned to shock as I turned over my straight.

Now before you get your religious nerves all tied up in a bundle, I wasn't playing some high stakes game like you see in a James Bond movie. I probably cleared 50 bucks. Nor is this really even about my brilliant poker playing. It's about the set-up.

I worked hard to read emotions as the cards came out, to listen to his cues that this was probably his last hand, to know he was a bit desperate at that moment to finish feeling good. Using all that info, I played him. I let him think he was probably in the lead as the cards were being dealt. I pressed him a bit about how fun his Vegas stay had been, win or lose. And he was mine…

What I didn't realize was I was being played as well. There was a more sinister force at work in that casino than my cheap psychology. I didn't notice it until I began to pull all the chips towards my side of the table. Much to the dealer's dismay, the pile included a decorative 3x5 card buried underneath the chips.

It was a pre-paid invitation to a party at the Pink Taco nightclub at the Hard Rock Casino. It was an invitation for escape… an invitation to feel good for a while… an invitation to participate in something a pastor of a 4000-member church could never do without getting caught… and it looked more valuable at that moment than any chips coming my way.

"I figured you earned it, doc," my English friend said.

"I'm leaving tonight and won't be going, but rest assured there was plenty of FUN in that place last weekend when I was there."

Everyone chuckled, the dealer chided him for messing with the table, and the sound of ping-pong balls rattled with hurricane force in my head.

Should I or shouldn't I? I've never had a chance like this. No one would ever know. It's not like other guys don't do it all the time.

But you have a commitment to your wife and your son and your daughter and your faith...

You get the point. It is during these defining moments of our lives that what should be an obvious choice is somehow obscured to equitable choice. Either way produces seemingly wanted rewards and unwanted consequences. There are times when our seemingly unshakeable values collide with insurmountable temptations. When our immovable convictions collide with unstoppable opportunities. There are times when one desire pushes against another and one will conquer while the other will cower.

Then it happened. Something in me, much clearer than the voices bouncing around in my head, something more tangible than the aching on the surface of my soul, it came from a place much deeper. It was the strongest whisper, the most confident command, and the gentlest push I have ever known.

"Eric, this is your moment. You must choose. When this

season of your life passes what do you want to be known for? Even when life is at its worst, you still have the ability to choose."

"I'll just take the chips, thanks," I spoke with the countenance of someone who had just won a lot more than a few bucks.

You may be reading this and *still* be hung up on the fact that I was in a casino playing poker. If so, you are totally missing the point. My defining moment is not your defining moment. You will have the opportunity to choose as well. It may happen in the workplace, the school yard, the neighborhood, or the internet. For you it may be a choice between life or death… faithfulness or infidelity… standing up or bowing down… honor or shame. It always comes. And it seems to happen when life already is piling on hurt, heartache, and disillusionment.

As I left the MGM that night, something in me knew I would survive the next six weeks without my wife. Even more so, something in me knew my love for her was going to be stronger than pending temptation. We were in this together, even though we were separate.

My mistake was believing that this defining moment meant the end of the refining moments.[10] But defining moments are just that—moments. Refining is a process that partners with pain and pressure in order to produce excellence. And Lord knows, I still have a lot of refining ahead of me…

Pray this:

Oh God[11]
Though I am allowed to approach you
I am not unmindful of my sins,
I do not deny my guilt,
I confess my wickedness, and earnestly plead forgiveness.
May I, with Moses, choose affliction
rather than enjoy the pleasures of sin.
Help me to place myself always under your guiding and
guardian care, to take firmer hold of the sure covenant that
binds me to you to feel more of the purifying, dignifying, soften-
ing influence of the religion I profess,
to have more compassion, love, empathy, courtesy,
to deem it an honor to be employed by you as an
instrument in your hands ready to seize every opportunity of
usefulness, and willing to offer all my talents to your service…

Ponder this:

"Character may be manifested in the great moments, but it is manufactured in the small ones."

– **Winston Churchill**

"I decide to do good, but I don't really do it; I decide not to do bad, but then I do it anyway. My decisions, such as they are, don't result in actions. Something has gone wrong deep within me and gets the better of me every time.

It happens so regularly that it's predictable. The moment I decide to do good, sin is there to trip me up. I truly delight in God's commands, but it's pretty obvious that not all of me joins in that delight. Parts of me covertly rebel, and just when I least expect it, they take charge.

I've tried everything and nothing helps. I'm at the end of my rope. Is there no one who can do anything for me? Isn't that the real question?

The answer, thank God, is that Jesus Christ can and does. He acted to set things right in this life of contradictions where I want to serve God with all my heart and mind, but am pulled by the influence of sin to do something totally different."

– Paul @Romans 7:19-25 (MSG)

Believe this:

I am willing to be honest enough to admit there is a war going on around my life and inside of my soul. I feel the tension and the opportunity daily to compromise what I know to be true and best for my life. The war seems overwhelming and out of my control, so today I focus on the battle in front of me. Today's battle has an outcome that I can influence. Whether it is a defining moment or a refining process I don't have to know. Regardless, today I choose life… I choose honor… I choose the higher road.

Chapter 7

Saying Goodbye without Christian Cheez-Whiz

"Boys and old men lie in the gutters of the streets,
my young men and women killed in their prime.
Angry, you killed them in cold blood,
cut them down without mercy.
"You invited, like friends to a party,
men to swoop down in attack
so that on the big day of God's wrath no one would get away.
The children I loved and reared—gone, gone, gone."
- **Jeremiah @Lamentations 2:21-22 (MSG)**

Every day I read Karen's Facebook posts. They tend to be like opening a window during a thunderstorm. During a storm, I can see the black clouds shattered by lightning and feel the rumbling aftershock of thunder, but somehow opening the window also provides the aroma of something fresh and new.

Karen's posts are like that. Perhaps because she is going through an intense storm in her life, and though mine is altogether different, it is also altogether the same, in the rumbling and terror it has potential to cause. Karen has been struggling to suppress a tumor lodged just above her hypothalamus for almost three years. Initially the clinics she went to told her the headaches and dizziness were "all in her head" and probably the result of her past drug use.

How ironic is that?

Karen came to my church years ago seeking restoration in her life. The victim of abuse, abandonment, and addiction, all she had left were two fatherless boys and a newborn girl for whom she wanted to provide a different future. She experienced first hand the power of God to take broken things and make them whole. The ensuing years were nothing but miracle upon miracle and grace upon grace in her life—the power of recovery, the embrace of community, the forgiveness of God. At least until the headaches started…

Being below poverty and on a fixed income doesn't provide the best of care for most Americans, and Karen is no exception. So the misdiagnoses went on and on for way too long, until a near coma sent her to a higher quality hospital where they discovered the tumor. Then the local newspaper picked up the story. Now she was the media's miracle woman who was granted a radical brain surgery to remove the tumor.

After surgery and countless hours of therapy, she seemed to have her life back, her daughter back, and two now-grown boys to visit. It was time to continue rebuilding the life she had almost lost a second time. Everything was back on track for Karen. Then the headaches started again…

It is during this season that Karen's Facebook popularity began to blossom. Three, four, sometimes six or more, posts a day about life's beauty, God's goodness, and her thankfulness for friends. She posted YouTube worship songs, pictures of friends and family, poetry and prayers. Just recently, when her birthday rolled around, she posted invites to all her Facebook friends to come over for a "fruit smoothie" party.

Who celebrates a birthday with fruit smoothies? Give me cake!

For Karen it was smoothies because at that time she had gone months with a feeding tube stuffed down her throat. It irritated her, interfered with her ability to speak and be a mom, and yet was a necessity due to the tumor's impinging influence on her ability to swallow. So it was, every post like a fresh breeze reminding me that even during storms there is beauty somewhere.

Then I got the call this week that Karen had lost her three-year battle with that vile brain tumor. I was stunned. I really believed, along with many others, that those tumorous clouds would part for her and she would again be reunited as a whole mother for her seven-year-old daughter and grown boys.

How could this be?

I can hear the voices already, "Oh wait… Dr. E, you don't understand. She is whole now with Jesus."

No, no I don't mean whole with Jesus, I mean whole—like a mommy with skin on for her daughter.

"She hasn't lost the battle, she has won! She is in heaven now. Death has lost its sting! Hallelujah!"

I know ultimately she lives eternally, but she lost her battle with cancer. I can't spin it any other way. As a single mom, with poverty-level income, she just couldn't afford the best treatments and doctors. The tumor was staved off for a while, but ultimately it took her life.

"Jesus promises to be a father to the fatherless, so her daughter will be okay."

Really? It was her mother that died. That little girl has hardly known her father—he was in prison and now is trying to get his life back together.

Okay, maybe if I didn't know Karen so well. Maybe if I hadn't been a part of her coming out of an addiction and abusive relationships, such spiritual platitudes would help me feel better. But right now, they have as much substance and nutrition to heal my heart as the Cheez-Whiz I sprayed on a Ritz cracker this afternoon.

Sometimes pain just hurts. Sometimes loss is really loss, not blessing disguised as loss. Sometimes grieving is like a hole torn open in your gut, so an evil hand can reach in and wretch out a piece of your soul. Pray all the healing balm you like, pain still hurts. The balm will aid in the healing, but first pain must be felt—not placated with slogans or anesthetized with chemicals.

I just can't believe the wretchedness life sometimes causes. I started this chapter last week not knowing the outcome of Karen's story, but filled with inspiration because of it. She didn't know how quickly the end would come, but that just didn't seem to matter. What mattered was she wanted to worship something greater than herself, she held a hope that this life really isn't all there is, and she understood that despite her current difficulties, her life had already been redeemed of so much pain that even an insidious tumor couldn't take away her joy. Next week, I will have the honor of facilitating her memorial service complete with a smoothie reception afterwards.

Pray this:

God, I admit sometimes life doesn't make sense. I know it rains on the just and the unjust alike, but my sense of fairness interferes with my faith. Help me to be a blessing to others, regardless of my understanding of the bigger story. Help me to believe there is goodness, even when all I see is darkness. Help me to be thankful for what I have, not for what I have not.

Ponder this:

Why is it more natural to blame God for the bad things that happen and take credit ourselves for the good that happens? What about the devil or just life—shouldn't they get some blame? Is it possible growing up in a culture of chemicals, pollution, and junk food may just be taking a toll on our bodies? Does God owe us perfect health when we don't live for it?

We must accept finite disappointment, but never lose infinite hope.

- Martin Luther King, Jr.

Believe this:

As painful as things are this season in my life, I choose to find a way to encourage someone else today. My life can make a difference even if it seems unnoticed by others. I can make excuses why I can't, or I can make an effort while I can.

Chapter 8

Trying to Hold
What Can't Be Held

My bed
has been floating forty days and nights
On the flood of my tears.
My mattress is soaked, soggy with tears.
The sockets of my eyes are black holes;
nearly blind, I squint and grope.
- David @Psalm 6:6-7 (MSG)

Perhaps the sizzle you hear in the frying pan of my heart is because my soul just hasn't had time to cool down during this season of losses in my life. We all suffer loss. It is part of living. Even with the passing of my very dear grandparents three years ago, I've realized how difficult it can be to try to hold onto something that just can't be held.

I realize the memories, the pictures and birthday trinkets are always available to stir up warm fuzzy feelings, but sometimes they seem like such poor substitutes for one of Grandma's famous hugs or "it'll be all right" smiles. Even the sounds generated by High-Def past family videos don't seem to fill the room like Grandpa's deep rumbling voice once did as he laughed during a game of Yahtzee with his grandkids.

Even toward the end of my grandparents' lives, when functions were slowing down and thought processes were a struggle, they continued to share something with each other that shapes my life today just as much as the Bible stories they read to me influenced me as a child.

Psalm 23

The LORD is my shepherd, I lack nothing.
He makes me lie down in green pastures,
he leads me beside quiet waters,
he refreshes my soul.
He guides me along the right paths
for his name's sake.
Even though I walk
through the darkest valley,
I will fear no evil,
for you are with me;
your rod and your staff,
they comfort me...
—David @Psalm 23:1-4 (NIV)

Honestly, I had to cut and paste this from Biblegateway.com, because I don't have it memorized. My grandparents recited it to each other most every evening during their 65 years of marriage (maybe that's why they lasted over 65 years). Even when Grandpa was struggling with the final stages of Alzheimer's, this verse—this truth—remained so ingrained in his mind and into his marriage that the dark valley of the unknown was not enough to steal his joy or his love for his Lord or his wife. It seemed to have helped carry them to the promised land...together.

Still Grandma and Grandpa were old. They had seen many good years and left a legacy to follow. I miss them, like I know many of you miss the elders in your life who have passed. It is so hard to let go of those whom we so dearly want to hold on to. Perhaps growing up with Disney's Lion King, I understood there is the great circle of life and their passing would someday occur. But knowing is one thing, actually accepting is another. I learned that with my grandparents. Then, just about a year later on July 4, 2010 I realized that accepting is only the beginning. Some loss takes us to a whole new depth where mere acceptance opens the door to either emotional crumbling or divine desperation....

Fourth of July in Las Vegas, Nevada is a lot of fun. The weather is guaranteed to be near 100 blistering-but-dry-and-sunny degrees (38 Celcius for my Canadian friends). The local casinos love to compete with each other, blasting their own fireworks high above the shimmering lights of the strip. So the evening is filled with eight or nine firework displays at one time celebrating our nation's freedom. All one needs is the perfect vantage point to celebrate the day—and we had it.

Due to a massive amount of foreclosures in Vegas at the time, rental properties were easy and affordable to come by. We rented a home complete with rock faced swimming pool, outdoor BBQ, and a deck that looked out over the entire Las Vegas strip. It was like living in a beer commercial and was perfect for sharing with friends.

In preparation for the afternoon and evening festivities, I was busy cleaning the pool and Cindy was feverishly marinating what seemed like a whole cow when the phone rang. It was some of our best friends who were coming over for the afternoon. Both of our families had recently relocated to Vegas, and we were a perfect fit together. They had three kids and we had two, though our oldest was in California. We shared faith, family fun, and food together all the time. Tonight we had planned to partake in all three in excess, until the phone rang…

"Cindy, this is Kenny. Please come over right away and watch the kids," Click. The phone went silent.

Cindy told me that was a bit odd of a phone call, but Kenny sounded serious so we better get over there. Besides, our son Carter had spent the night at their place hangin' out with their oldest boy. We could pick him up, so he could help us get ready for the evening.

As we approached Kenny and Trina's home I was stunned by the flashing lights bouncing to and from the three police cars and fire truck crowding the front of their home. As I pulled up, I began to get a horrible feeling in my stomach. Then my eyes focused on the back seat of one police car where I saw my dear friend Kenny sitting with a glazed look over his eyes.

Before my mind could fully register the image I heard my wife cry out, "Trina is in the back seat of that police car!"

I pulled over and hesitated for a moment before opening the door. I knew something horrible awaited me if I got out, but what? I wanted to reboot, go back, and start the day over… but couldn't.

Thankfully, my adrenaline kicked my brain into gear and my previous training as a support officer for the fire department kicked in. I went straight to the officer who was in charge, introduced myself, and explained why I was there. He told me there had been an accident and until they could get all the information straight, the husband and wife needed to be separated.

"Regardless of the accident, my wife really needs to be in that car with Trina. Is that okay?" I asked.

"Normally that is against protocol, but I can tell these are really good people, so I'll let her sit with her until we get some things figured out."

From there I went inside and was confronted by more officers and paramedics. My mind was spinning, my heart was racing, yet I felt like I was in some sort of dream.

Wake up, Eric… Wake up… Just rewind and reboot and start this day over…

I was told Trinity, their daughter, was at a friend's house, and that the two older boys (my son and Kenny's older son, Josiah) were upstairs. That only left 15-month-old Jude unacounted for.

One, two, three kids accounted for. Good. Where's Jude? Oh my God, it's Jude… reboot… please reboot…

"I'm afraid that the youngest child, Jude, is at the hospital. There has been a horrible accident and it appears he crawled into the back yard and fell in the pool," came a voice that was barely audible to my already overwhelmed senses.

"As soon as we are confident it was only an accident we will release the parents to the hospital to be with him."

No wonder Kenny and Trina looked so dazed and trapped inside those cars. They needed to be with their son. Reboot… come on… reboot…

The next three days became a blur for all involved. Jude was in a coma, we were in shock, and the infant ICU was in full-time crisis mode. Never before had I prayed so hard with so much faith. Never before had our friends and those connected via Facebook, e-mail, and Twitter prayed with such fervency. We believed Jude was a miracle from his birth and it just didn't seem possible this was happening just 15 months later.

Jude wasn't supposed to be here. Without going into all the details, when a child is born two years after the father's vasectomy, in response to brother and sister's pestering God for a little brother, and all via a very difficult pregnancy— you begin to sense there must be something special about this child. And he was.

Even by 15 months he was showing signs of his daddy's musical giftedness, his brother's goofiness, his sister's laugh, and his mommy's passion to worship. He seemed to be all things toddler and just a little more.

Reboot… this isn't happening… Jude has a destiny… it can't be over before it has even begun…

July 7 came upon us like the dark cloud of inevitability. Decisions regarding life support had to be made. Jude was showing no signs of progress and even some signs of brain deterioration. It was time to let him go.

- But how does one let go of someone in whom every fiber of your being is screaming to hold?
- How does one actually make the decision to end the physical life of someone whom they hold so dear, even knowing there is an afterlife waiting?
- How does one actually step across that threshold of decision?

They did it the same way Karen found a way, the same way my grandparents found a way.

"Even though I walk through the darkest valley, I will fear no evil, for you are with me…"

Kenny and Trina are some of the bravest people I have ever met. They choose to worship. Not just listen to music mind you—worship. It is an attitude not a platitude. We filled the room with worship music that drove past religion straight into reality. Just as Jude was disconnected from the machines he was laid between mom and dad and reconnected with those who had given him life. I sat in a corner and wept some of the deepest tears I have ever wept, knowing that the pain I was experiencing was only a fraction of the depth being experienced on their hospital bed at that moment.

Yet… shalom was present. There was something… no someone… as tangibly present for good in that room as there was the grief of loss.

The year that followed has not been easy for my friends Kenny, Trina, Josiah, and Trinity. Nor will the years that follow this one. There will always be a hole, a missing heart-shaped piece of that household. Yet, instead of emotionally crumbling, they are trying to remain divinely desperate. Not a day goes by Trina doesn't wish she could stop… reboot… start over… Instead they are learning to stop… refocus… take it one day further.

Not long after leaving the hospital broken and numb, I received this long text from one of the ER nurses:

"My name is Sally and I was working at St. Rose the day Jude came to the ER and also with him Wednesday July 7th. I have been working in the medical field for over 10 years and have seen a lot of sadness over the years. I am a mother of two young children and Jude reminded me of my own son. I think over the years you build a wall so that you are not affected by the tragedies you see, but for some reason I was really impacted by Jude's untimely death and the impact I know it will have on his parents. Maybe because I am a parent or just human, I think of his family often since that day and I pray for them all the time. I think I am a better parent these days because of Jude. I hope and pray each day that the pain will somehow subside for his family…"

Yep, Kenny and Trina are some of the bravest people I know. Then again, so was Karen, and my grandparents. With all the loss these past couple years, sometimes I wonder if I'll make it.

Then I remember I have some footsteps to follow. I have some choices I can make. I want to end up a brave worshipper, not a frail shell, when I finish this journey. Thanks for setting an example for all of us, you five. In the midst of the darkest valleys you've reminded us there is always a ray of hope.

Pray this:

Oh, only for so short a while you
have loaned us to each other,
because we take form in your act of drawing us,
and we take life in your painting us,
and we breathe in your singing us.
But only for so short a while
have you loaned us to each other.
Because even a drawing cut in obsidian fades,
and the green feathers, the crown feathers,
of the Quetzal bird lose their color,
and even the sounds of the waterfall

die out in the dry season.
So, we too, because only for a short while
have you loaned us to each other.
—Aztec Indian Prayer

Ponder this:

The will of God is never exactly what you expect it to be. It may seem to be much worse, but in the end it's going to be a lot better and a lot bigger.

—Elisabeth Elliot[12]

Believe this:

I choose to recognize that I have been given a gift: a gift to grieve and be thankful at the same time.

I will embrace the waves of each as they come.

I will not isolate from safe people around me, nor put pressure on myself to be more than I am capable of during this time in my life.

I give myself permission to hurt and slow down, even as I understand for others, the world may go on.

Chapter 9

Even When It's Messy

Will the Lord walk off and leave us for good?
Will he never smile again?
Is his love worn threadbare?
Has his salvation promise burned out?
Has God forgotten his manners?
Has he angrily stalked off and left us?
"Just my luck," I said. "The High God goes out of business
just the moment I need him."
- unknown person @Psalm 77:7-10 (MSG)

When Sandy and I started our tattoo website a few years back, we were stunned by the number of "memorial" tattoos that were submitted. Losing loved ones, losing friends, losing pets... it doesn't matter. The grieving and the pain experienced can be life altering. Perhaps the only difference lies in how deep that pain actually goes. Still pain is pain, loss is loss, tears are tears... It is something we all share in common with our human condition. But grief isn't always grief in the ways Western culture has taught us.

Grief can be messy. Despite what we have been taught, it seldom is organized into neat little stages and categories. What is important is that we actually grieve. And we need to be in places where we are given permission to hurt, be numb, have faith one day, and doubt the next.

Friends, family, churches, or whomever, need to slow down and let life happen. We live in such an anesthetizing culture, where pain is bad and numbness is good, that we tend to jump on "moving people along in the process" like a bunch of well-meaning piranha—usually because their pain makes us uncomfortable.

People these days just don't like messes or simply don't know how to handle them. People who are in a mess, pick up on that vibe and tend to avoid the added discomfort of not being "well enough, soon enough" and thus get isolated.

Few things are harder on healing a wounded heart than isolation, but few things are more awkward than trying to help a friend who is in pain and suffering from the dizziness of grief without knowing what to do. Somehow they seem to work against each other like some divine conspiracy to derail future healing and friendships.

Here are two things to keep in mind when walking alongside those who are grieving:

Don't just sit there doing nothing: I don't know how many times I've talked to people in well meaning home Bible studies or civic groups who have heard of a friend who is grieving and they just say, "I just didn't know what to say or do, so I ended up doing nothing."

The Amish have a phrase for that: "The smallest deed done 'tis better than the noblest promise forgotten."

One thing I've learned from healthy recovery/addiction groups is the immediate and consistent follow-up on the "missing." Not like a Branch Davidian cult, but like a "hey, I've been there and I'm here to help" friend. Consider your boundaries and their boundaries. The closer you've been in the good life, the closer you should probably be in grief life. Your touch (literal or figuratively) should be in proportion to what has been normal prior to the loss.

Don't be afraid to talk about the loved one who is gone. Sometimes real healing comes through sharing stories of remembrance. Even with the loss of Jude and its grief that went so deep, Trina, Kenny, and I became aware how seldom people would use Jude's name in a sentence. It was more awkward to talk "around" the subject of that precious child than it was to talk about him. Use discretion, but shared memories often lend themselves to shared healing.

During this season of losing loved ones, I have found my life buoyed as much by distant acquaintances sending a post card or posting on Facebook note as those who kept handing me Kleenexes trying to keep my sleeve being a one-armed handkerchief. Life puts a good balance of people around us who are there to share a portion of the burden, even when those pieces of our life seem shattered across the floor.

Just sit there and do nothing: I know this sounds like a contradiction to what I just mentioned, but hang with me for a moment. There is an ancient Jewish custom of bereavement called Sitting Shiva. Though the details are significant and purposeful for those who practice it within the Jewish faith, the principle is very important for us all. *Shiva* is about allowing time and space to embrace death. It gives one's soul time to simultaneously let go of a loved one and hold on to memories. As well, it gives place for close family and friends to aid in that process.

At its core, Shiva is about doing nothing for seven days. I don't know if you've lost someone you care deeply about—maybe, like Trina, it was a child, maybe, like me, it was a relative, maybe, like you, it was losing a spouse or a life-long friend. Regardless of the *who*, it is the *what* that becomes so debilitating.

Everything seems like an effort to get accomplished—laundry, cooking, paying bills, even getting out of bed. Emotions ebb and flow like a forceful tide overwhelming one's sense of being and motivation. Then to top it off, the grieving person begins to get buried under all the "shoulds" they aren't accomplishing, especially when guests are present. That's why *Shiva* becomes so important.

It is about just sitting with the one who is closest to the grieving and just being, not doing. Being next to someone in pain and saying nothing is better than being with someone and doing the wrong anything. Shiva is about letting the one who hurts the most guide the being and the doing for the seven days, but they don't have to be or do alone. You are there, like a silent but ever-present friend, not interfering with grief but facilitating it.

Pray this:

Dear God,

At the very least, perhaps my own pain and grief will give me greater empathy to those around me who are hurting. Will you help me to be willing to reach outside of my own struggle and share a moment with another in need? You have the answers, I just need compassion and sensitivity. Help me to be a good listener when needed, supportive when warranted, and present in mind and heart always.

Ponder this:

The friend who can be silent in a moment of despair or confusion, who can stay steadfast in an hour of grief, who can tolerate not knowing, not curing, not healing and face the reality of powerlessness, that is a friend who cares.

—**Henri Nouwen**, author

I'll never forget the trouble, the utter lostness,
the taste of ashes, the poison I've swallowed.
I remember it all—oh, how well I remember—
the feeling of hitting the bottom.
But there's one other thing I remember,
and remembering, I keep a grip on hope:
God's loyal love couldn't have run out,
his merciful love couldn't have dried up.
They're created new every morning.
How great your faithfulness!
I'm sticking with God (I say it over and over).
He's all I've got left.
- Jeremiah @Lamentations 3:19-24 (MSG)

Believe this:

Silence does not have to be uncomfortable when the space is filled with compassion and peace. Sharing stories is not digging up wounds when tempered with love and respect. In my pain, I choose to be open to sharing both silence and story with those who are safe to me. In the pain of others, I choose to be available to do the same. I recognize I need others as much as I need God through this valley of darkness.

Chapter 10

Lean on Me

He ground my face into the gravel.
He pounded me into the mud.
I gave up on life altogether.
I've forgotten what the good life is like.
I said to myself, "This is it. I'm finished.
God is a lost cause."
— Jeremiah @Lamentations 3:16-18 (MSG)

"To the world you may be just one person, but to one person
you may be the world."
— various authors @quotegarden.com

"If you live to be 100, I hope I live to be 100 minus 1 day, so I
never have to live without you."
— Winnie the Pooh @quotegarden.com

*"This is my wish for you: Comfort on difficult days, smiles when
sadness intrudes, rainbows to follow the clouds, laughter to kiss
your lips, sunsets to warm your heart, hugs when spirits sag,
beauty for your eyes to see, friendships to brighten your being,
faith so that you can believe, confidence for when you doubt,
courage to know yourself, patience to accept the truth, love to
complete your life."*
—cheesy quote @quotegarden.com

Okay, so maybe on the right day when I'm in the right mood even the aforementioned quotes could provide a few warm fuzzies down my ice cold spine. But not this year… not even last year… nope. Today, they just seem empty and hollow. Like words without a soul. I know they are trying to tell me something, but such platitudes can't seem to find enough volume to overcome the noise my life is making. Ironically, there have been people who hardly spoke a word, but whose behaviors have transcended what seemed to be the clanging disintegration of my life.

Having moved out of our soon-to-be-foreclosed-upon home in SoCal into a temporary rental across town, I was striving to settle into a new job and a more permanent rental three hours away in Las Vegas (if you are counting that's three moves in two months). Being in Vegas, I felt we were finally getting some distance between the nightmare created by the mortgage/banking fiasco and the sucking sound that nearly evaporated my bank account.

We were diligently beating our heads up against a wall trying to get our home short-sold prior to the banks seemingly random foreclosure deadline. The bank had "misplaced" our paperwork a second time and our real estate agent found herself becoming more of a mortgage lawyer than a sales person. Regardless, we wanted out from underneath this all-consuming frustration and emotionally draining experience, so we tried our best to stay focused. Then it happened…

My wife drove to SoCal for the weekend in order pack our belongings from our temporary rental and tie up more loose ends with the potential sale of our house. While there she drove by our old home to check on it. Though the circumstances had become a nightmare, it once was a dream home for us. Simple by California standards, yet perfect for our family.

She unlocked the front door, let herself in, and then immediately felt a rush of fear and anxiety overwhelm her. There, in the empty house, was a pile of trash and a broken dining room window. Someone had broken the window, unlatched its slider, and had been "partying" in our absence. She called me in Vegas…

"Someone broke into our house and left a bunch of trash. What do I do?" she said with a barely audible voice.

"Get out now. Call the police and we will have to have someone come board up the window," came as controlled of a response as I could give considering the absolute rage and disbelief that was welling up within me.

Will this house issue ever go away? I screamed inside.

"Why? Why does this have to keep happening to us?" was my wife's tear-filled questioned.

Cindy mustered what little emotional energy she had left, filed a police report, and had someone come over to board up the window. Crisis over.

Pause the story for a moment…

Have you been in such a place?

Maybe not regarding a house, but your job…or your health…or your kids…or your life?

Those moments when things just seem to be going from bad to worse?

When you are trying your best to cope with a wound and get back on your feet, then some sinister force seems to pour salt on your raw emotions inflaming them almost beyond tolerance?

Unfortunately, that day for my wife was just the wound; the salt came the next day.

The following morning, after the police report and after the window repair had been done, she stopped by again to see if everything was cleaned up. As she opened the front door, a breeze blew across her face. A breeze only caused by air being drawn from one opening in a house to another. As her eyes focused across the room toward the back kitchen and patio door, her body went limp. In retaliation for the boarded window, our culprit had thrown a cinder block through the rear patio door shattering the glass and sending shards all over the hardwood floor. That brick might have well been thrown at her… unable to breathe, unable to slow her racing heart, unable to see straight… she collapsed.

Finally, she mustered enough strength to call my cell phone.

"I can't do this anymore. I can't handle this. Why? Why does everything have to go so wrong?"

I could feel the tears through my cell phone as she tried to tell me what had just happened.

There I was in Las Vegas, my wife in pain in SoCal, and I felt paralyzed. I couldn't leave a job that I had barely started training for, besides there was no way I could get there in time to help her stand up or clean up the mess. I couldn't call the FBI and put out an APB on the SOB that just violated my home and my wife's emotional stability. I was pinned down with my own frustration and anger. So I did the only thing I knew how to do… I called a friend.

Here's the thing about friendship: *What you sow into them during the mundane days of life will ultimately bear fruit when the traumatic days come.* That's why so many of our superficial friendships end up being superficially supportive when we need them most. In other words, we reap what we sow.

Haven't you experienced it? You hang out with buddies in the office, talk around the water-cooler, and chat about NFL drafts and ESPN highlights. But when tragedy hits the fan, often their response is in proportion to your investment—maybe a nice card, a visit at the hospital, or a Facebook comment.

Or perhaps it's your church Bible study group or Kiwanis friends. Those people who you feel connected to and really like, but then you don't show up for a week or two, or a month or two, and not even a phone call? What's up with that?

Could there be a difference between shared activities together and a shared life together?

Before we go pointing fingers at all those insensitive people, we must remember it often goes back to what you and I were sowing into those relationships that determines what we got out of them.

I called my friends Steve and Richard. My voice was cracking with anger and pain. Without hesitation, almost as if it were his own wife in pain, Steve said he'd be there and do whatever it took to make things better. Richard's response echoed the same commitment. My heart breathed just a little easier and my anger receded a bit.

Here's the odd part. Even though I was no longer a part of their church, I knew in my soul I was still a part of their lives. It was because we hadn't just done church together, we had done life together. The countless nights hangin' out barbecuing, sharing stories, and helping fix each other's stuff were the seeds that had been sown into this moment—the moment I needed a friend.

Maybe that's why it was so natural to spend three days at the hospital with Kenny and Trina as tragedy overtook their lives. Maybe that's why certain people just seem to rise above the norm during crisis or absence, while others seem to fade into the distance. It has something to do with Faith, Food, and Fantasy. Indeed it is about a shared life, not just shared activity.

When we share a common belief in the purpose of life (faith), share the mundane times of life (like meals), and learn to share the dreams and hopes we have (fantasy), seeds are planted that bear fruit seasons later.

I'm not dissing superficial friendship or virtual friendships. Those definitely have a place in our lives, too. My life has been encouraged too many times from responses of people I hardly know as I've posted struggles or thoughts online. And for many of those people, I have a sense that if they were near they would also be dear. The virtual world has connected us in ways that were impossible a generation ago.

The question is: *Has this new reality broadened the reach of what friendship is or diluted it down to a number and "likes" on a webpage?*

(Rabbit trail: How odd, as I was sitting here in my fav local coffee shop, Jives, just typing away, the barista and I had a conversation regarding our friendship status on Facebook. She and I are now "friends"! However, she was really bummed that an old guy like me actually had more friends than her. In my best Yoda wisdom I responded, "One friend on the ground is often better than one-hundred in cyber space."

She responded, "Yeah, but I still can't believe you are more popular than me!"

Maybe she will read this book and get it. But in the meantime, make sure and friend me on Facebook, cuz I want to stay ahead of her... LOL :-))

In my life, it seems I need both. I love to connect with people on a broad field of ideas and mediums, but without a few solid people in my life who know my secrets, are more committed to my character than my gifting, I'd be a mess.

We are like Legos. Each of us connects in different ways. You may be like me—that wide, thin, green platform piece where just about any other Lego can find a place to connect. But if I'm not careful my life can become a mile wide and a quarter-inch deep. Even I need solid connections with others.

Or maybe you are like my wife—the colorful building block type. She doesn't connect with lots of people at once, but when you are connected to her… you are connected to her. She brings to friendships a strength and stability that is good at holding things together. Access sometimes may feel limited, but stability is strong.

Of course you could be one of those specialty pieces—you know the ones that when you pick them up you ask yourself, "What in the world is this for?" Then after a while of creating your Lego masterpiece, that item… that odd spinning one-nob doo-dad, becomes the thing that takes your creation from just blah to brilliant.

The point is we all need to be connected. And as my time of unraveling has felt more chronic than limited in scope, those connections help keep me grounded in reality. If you are finding yourself in crisis now, nurture what friendships you have and don't try to expect more out of some people than they are willing to give. Isolation breeds further disillusionment; connection fosters strength.

If your life is currently in cruise control, then use your time wisely. Actually evaluate the seeds you are sowing into your current friendships. Are they simply friendships of convenience or of substance?

Are you finding it natural to share life or just activities? If you're not sure, do something radical and ask. Nothing shakes up a humdrum Bible study like someone choosing to be real and transparent about their lives.

Speaking of the Bible, there are numerous examples of friendships throughout God's story: David and Jonathan, Moses and Joshua, Jesus and John. But there is a rather obscure passage that tends to be used more in wedding ceremonies than in home invasions. Which is odd because it is really less about love and tulips; and more about death, disillusionment, and despair. It's the story of three women: Orpah, Naomi, and Ruth.

> *Once upon a time—it was back in the days when judges led Israel—there was a famine in the land.*
>
> — **@Ruth 1:1 (MSG)**

I can't even get past the first verse of the story without relating. It begins with a great famine in the land, a time of utter hardship. Provision had ceased; the apparent blessing of God seemed to have dried up like a raisin in the sun.

Have you experienced the sudden shift from affluence to borderline poverty? Have you wondered where the blessing disappeared to?

In this situation the husband, Elimelech, moves his wife, Naomi, and their two sons to a foreign land in order to find provision and hope. They were desperate and grasping for anything. While in the foreign land both sons marry foreign women and then things go downhill from there. Over the course of 10 years, Naomi's husband dies and then both of her sons die. Naomi is left in a foreign land with two daughters-in-law and nothing else.

Don't just read this as a Sunday school story... her husband died, both of her sons died. How could she not help but feel abandoned by God and life? Especially in ancient times, to be a widow was pretty much a sentence to poverty and/or prostitution for survival.

Not until these days have I understood the pile-up effect of loss. Just when it seems things can't get worse, they seem to slip a little more. Naomi was lost and frustrated and hurting and scared. If you have been there or are there today, read on...

One day she got herself together, she and her two daughters-in-law, to leave the country of Moab and set out for home... After a short while on the road, Naomi told her two daughters-in-law, "Go back. Go home and live with your mothers. And may God treat you as graciously as you treated your deceased husbands and me." ... She kissed them and they cried openly.

> *They said, "No, we're going on with you to your people."*
>
> *But Naomi was firm: "Go back, my dear daughters. Why would you come with me? ... Go back, dear daughters—on your way, please!... No, dear daughters; this is a bitter pill for me to swallow—more bitter for me than for you. God has dealt me a hard blow."*

> — @Ruth 1:6-13 (MSG)

Naomi sees no reason to stay in the foreign land and decides to venture back to her homeland. While on the road she realizes that she is dragging her two daughters-in-law away from their roots and tries to convince them to return. Some debating ensues, but there are tears. These women had shared a lot of loss together and they struggled with what to do next.

I've attended and facilitated a lot of funerals in my day. Whether it be the death of a spouse, a child, or a parent—one thing has become evident to me. Death of close family members can bring out the best and the worst in people. Yet we hardly ever talk about it.

Little stress fractures under the surface arise creating sharp pains and divisions during the grieving process, especially when money is involved.

You do understand that tragedy and pain can either bring you closer together as a family or tear you apart? It often depends on two important words: communication and humility.

In this situation, Naomi stops and communicates her desires for these two girls. She is honest about her own emotional frailty and fear of the future. They love her and want to continue, but also understand her reasoning. They cried openly…

Being able to laugh openly with friends is one thing; feeling secure enough to cry openly with friends is quite another. I know so many guys who share the Super Bowl and the Final Four games together, hike a mountain, or cap some terrorists on X-box, but can't even fathom who they would turn to in crisis. I know so many women who gladly gossip and whine about other people's problems, but feel so insecure they could never admit their own crisis with others. We reap what we sow…

Again they cried openly. Orpah kissed her mother-in-law good-bye; but Ruth embraced her and held on.

Naomi said, "Look, your sister-in-law is going back home to live with her own people and gods; go with her."

But Ruth said, "Don't force me to leave you; don't make me go home. Where you go, I go; and where you live, I'll live. Your people are my people, your God is my god; where you die, I'll die, and that's where I'll be buried, so help me God—not even death itself is going to come between us!"

When Naomi saw that Ruth had her heart set on going with her, she gave in. And so the two of them traveled on together to Bethlehem.

— @Ruth 1:14-19 (MSG)

Okay, get past the wedding bell romance so often contained in this passage for a moment. The significance is about three people who are friends. First there were three, then there were two. Orpah returned home and Ruth continued on.

But get this point: Orpah was not a *bad* person in Naomi's life, she was just a done person. They wept openly and then parted ways. No bitterness, no "how could you abandoned me?" No "Ruth must love me more." They traveled to that point as friends and then departed as friends.

Listen: *When some people walk out of your life, it is okay to let them go.*

They may not be bad people, just done people. Some of us spend so much time hanging onto past relationships, trying to prop them up and keep them active, that it fuels tensions and jealously in our current ones. Sometimes people come into our lives for a season, to bless us, to encourage us, to spur us on, but then the season ends and it's time to plant something new.

Some of us continue to hang onto past romances clear back in high school and college, only adding tension to the relationships God has right in front of us. Some of us hang onto past hurts from years ago—trying to fix what doesn't need fixed or understand what no longer can be understood. And such grasps backward only loosen our grip on present relationships today.

Perhaps it is because I have moved so many times in my life that I've learned this lesson. There are so many people I am thankful for as we have journeyed together for a season. So many people have impacted my life, but for a season. I love how technology enables me to stay connected with them, but not dependent on them for this part of my journey. There are those friendships that seem to naturally pick up where they left off and those friendships that I must allow room to have changed and grown in different directions.

We don't see Orpah again in Naomi's story. I suppose if Naomi would have had access to Facebook, Myspace, LinkedIn, Twitter, Flickr, and FriendFinder, things may have been different. But Naomi's life went on… Orpah's life went on… Ruth's life went on…

Now I can't help but see Sam-wise, Frodo's dearest friend from the Lord of the Rings series in Ruth. God put her there to help carry Naomi from a place of bitterness and despair to a place of wholeness and repair. Just as Sam-wise wasn't willing to leave Frodo's side even during the darkest parts of his story, Ruth felt deep within her spirit that part of her own destiny lie within helping Naomi.

When they arrived in Bethlehem the whole town was soon buzzing: "Is this really our Naomi? And after all this time!"

But she said, "Don't call me Naomi; call me Bitter. The Strong One has dealt me a bitter blow. I left here full of life, and God has brought me back with nothing but the clothes on my back. Why would you call me Naomi? God certainly doesn't. The Strong One ruined me."

And so Naomi was back, and Ruth the foreigner with her, back from the country of Moab. They arrived in Bethlehem at the beginning of the barley harvest…

— *@Ruth 1:19-22* **(MSG)**

All of the loss and disillusionment and pain had forced

a new identity upon Naomi. As she returned home, she no longer wanted to be called Noami, but "Bitter."

Yet Ruth remained by her side.

I know it's tough to be that kind of friend—when someone you care about is sliding into despair and you just can't seem to find the right words or do the right thing to help lift them up.

But Ruth remained…

I know it is difficult to try to help make sense out of senseless pain and hurt with someone you care about… but Ruth remained.

I understand how sometimes the labor of friendship goes long periods without much sense of appreciation… but Ruth remained. And in remaining she not only changed Naomi's life from one of bitterness to restoration, she changed her own life from poverty to provision. Yes, we reap what we sow.

Sometimes we need another person to believe in God's goodness for us. "Believe in my belief, until you can believe in your own…" is a common phrase my recovery friends use. Ruth had a connection with Naomi. She was drawn to this woman and chose to give up other relationships for it to continue.

In today's culture we have trouble with same gender relationships. We've been taught that we can only bond in the flesh. That's ridiculous. I've heard this Scripture and others twisted in totally inappropriate ways because of that.

There is a powerful force that can arise from life-giving, non-sexually or emotionally enmeshed, same gender friendships. The truth is:

- David and Jonathan bonded in spirit
- Paul and Timothy bonded in spirit
- Perhaps even Jesus' relationship with John was at that level.

It is frustrating that, in today's culture, it is becoming more and more difficult to develop healthy, life-giving same gender friendships.

Ones that don't become co-dependent ... emotionally enmeshed ... out of balance to other relationships. But when friendship is built on someone other than ourselves, it is possible.

These two were bonded in spirit. It was more than a mother/daughter thing, more than an emotional entanglement... It was about faithfulness and a covenant before God.

Now when you bond in the Spirit, God holds you to it... so don't make such covenants lightly.

As you read the rest of the story you'll see God's purpose and design behind it all. God used Naomi in Ruth's story and used Ruth in Naomi's story to pull them into the future HE had for each of them!

Walking a friend through crisis is hard work. But the first step is being sure you are the one to do the walking. Just ask any of my friends who give their lives to helping others out of addiction. Getting someone to a meeting, and spending seven days by their bedside as they detox are very different tasks. One is an Orpah and the other is a Ruth. Both significant, both valuable, but both require decisions about the cost involved.

Or ask my friend, Kap, who lived in my abandoned house to insure there were no other break-ins while we waited for it to be sold. Going from a successful realtor and man of faith to a homeless man who felt abandoned by God and others, he knew the pain of losing his own home during the real-estate collapse of 2009. Yet our friendship and our mutual willingness to be transparent in crisis led us to the having him "house-sit" while we tried to pick up the pieces of our shattered lives. His need for temporary housing intersected our need for temporary security at the place of genuine transparency.

Then there were the six guys who came over and helped this frustrated and disillusioned former pastor pack up a moving van with what was left of his belongings. Though they didn't necessarily agree with the decisions that had forced my departure, they were more concerned about easing my transition than having a Saturday to play in the Southern California sun. They gave me a day and then were done. As weird as it sounds—Kap was my Ruth, the guys were my Orpah, and together they provided a ray of hope to get me through another day.

And so in my Lego life, perhaps like yours, we've experienced a dismantling of all we held dear. Yet somehow, if we take time to look around, we find we are still connected in ways we didn't expect or value before. And when the re-building begins to occur, may we use those pieces to form a stronger foundation for the next storm that may come.

Pray this:

You have blessed us, O God,
with the gift of friendship,
the bonding of persons
in a circle of love.
We thank you for such a blessing:
for friends who love us,
who share our sorrows,
who laugh with us in celebration,
who bear our pain,
who need us as we need them,
who weep as we weep,
who hold us when words fail,
and who give us the freedom
to be ourselves.
Bless our friends with health,
wholeness, life, and love.
Amen.
— author unknown

Ponder this:

Friendship is unnecessary, like philosophy, like art... It has no survival value; rather it is one of those things that give value to survival.

- C. S. Lewis

Two people are better than one,
because they get more done by working together.
If one falls down,
the other can help him up.
But it is bad for the person who is alone and falls,
because no one is there to help.
- **King Solomon @Ecclesiastes 4:9-10 (NCV)**

Believe this:

Regardless of whether I feel my friendships are plenty or few, I choose to release with thankfulness those friendships whose season has come and gone, and sow appropriately into those friendships that remain.

I will not isolate from those whom God has put into my life to share my burdens, nor will I use my crisis as an excuse to shy away from helping them.

I choose to be transparent and honest with those who are safe and have boundaries with those who aren't.

Chapter 11

God in My Colon

Please, God, no more yelling,
no more trips to the woodshed.
Treat me nice for a change;
I'm so starved for affection.
Can't you see I'm black-and-blue,
beat up badly in bones and soul?
God, how long will it take
for you to let up?
- David @Psalm 6:1-3 (MSG)

What do former president Ronald Reagan, television celebrity Sharon Osbourne, and baseball great Darryl Strawberry all have in common? Colons. Actually, having overcome colon cancer to be exact.

What do legendary NFL coach Vince Lombardi, "Peanuts" cartoonist Charles Schultz, and actress beauty Audry Hepburn have in common? Colons again. Actually, more specifically, they each died of colon cancer.

I suppose that puts me in pretty famous company. But I'm just me, and along with almost twelve million people per year in the United States, I found out I had cancer.[13] Perhaps, you are just you—with a similar diagnosis.

Let's back up 14 days... As if it wasn't difficult enough

moving from SoCal to Las Vegas, from my dream job as a pastor to a 100-percent commission job selling timeshares, from finding my identity in helping others to viewing others as a commodity to help me. Now I didn't start my life journey planning toward timeshare sales, but at this stage of my life it was the best temporary option I had. I graciously took the sales offer from my long-time friend, Rod, who had become a V.P. at one of the nation's largest timeshare companies.

I woke up every day trying to be thankful knowing millions of other people were falling into unemployment quicker than the government could spend money to stop it. As if that wasn't a hard enough transition… my wife had to keep pushing me to get a colonoscopy—"because at least we have good health insurance right now."

I was having a hard time justifying getting a routine colonoscopy five years earlier than the recommended time for a fit and vigorous guy my age just to save a few bucks. But as every good husband does, I eventually acquiesced to my wife and made the appointment. Just a few days after my "Moon River" encounter[14], I was doing my thing selling timeshares when my cell phone rang, twice in the span of about 15 minutes. I was busy, so I let it go to voicemail.

Message One: "Hey Eric, this is Dr. Constantine. When you get a few minutes can you call me back? I want to chat with you about your colonoscopy results."

Message Two: "Mr. Sandras, this is Dr. Wiesz from the Nevada Digestive Disease Center. Please call my office as soon as possible. I'd like to speak with you about your results."

It's not like I've had a lot of experience with colonoscopies and such, but common sense told me that two calls within a few minutes of each other weren't to congratulate me on having a fine, top-of-the-line colon. I took a few deep breaths, found a secluded spot underneath some palm trees, and called my doc back.

Doc Constantine is one of the coolest doctors I've ever had. And up till this point I always listened to his advice— whether it was about supplements, cholesterol, or sunscreen. Maybe it is because he always made eye contact as he spoke in normal terms and not "doctorese."

So normally, I paid attention to every word and took his advice seriously. But this conversation was different. As he took a good 10 minutes on the phone with me explaining the results of my colonoscopy and how they had sent the results to two independent labs for verification, here's basically what I heard:

> *"blah...blah... blah... PRETTY SURE IT'S CANCER.... Blah, blah, blah... CANCER... blah... blah... blah... AGGRESSIVE FORM OF CANCER... blah... blah... blah... Can you come in tomorrow?"*

As I hung up the phone, I felt strangely dizzy. Thoughts began to rush into my mind faster than I could filter out faith from fear.

Oh come on God! Really? Isn't my life bad enough already?!

This has got to be a money making conspiracy between doctors because the economy is down...

Oh my God... how do I tell Cindy? Should I tell Cindy? Do I even want to tell Cindy? Of course, I have to tell Cindy, she's all I have for emotional support...

I can't afford to die... wait, I can't really afford to live...

If you've been through the diagnosis of any life threatening disease or event, you know how quickly the questions roll through your mind and then comes... numbness. Like a heavy fog on a cold, damp night beckoning you to tuck yourself under the warmth of a down comforter until it all goes away.

Here's what was wrong with the space Cindy and I were in—with the loss of our house, our savings, and realizing that I hadn't been employed long enough in my 100-percent commission job to qualify for disability pay—we found ourselves more concerned about finances than the reality of whether this cancer was going to take my life. How odd when money seems more important than relationship.

I've never been more thankful for my wife's gift of administration and business management. She took charge, while I drifted in and out of doctor's offices. The next few days were a blur of tests, re-tests, insurance company jousting, and finally setting up surgery. Before I knew it, my intestine was a foot shorter than it had ever been and I went from a full-fledged colon to a semi-colon in my body. And I was lucky, because I survived...

After all of my wife's prodding to get a colonoscopy, it was the very fact that I went in early that saved my life. Though the cancer they had found was very aggressive, it had just gotten started eating away at my life. It hadn't broken through the intestinal walls and thus hadn't invaded other parts of my body yet. The surgery took care of it all. And now all I had to do was repair the chaos the month and a half of surgery and recuperation had caused.

It was during that time of fear, disbelief, and further disillusionment that I found God in my colon. It was during those six weeks of darkness and my own crisis of faith that God found a way to shed a little ray of hope into my seemingly crumbling world. Maybe it is because during those times in our lives that everything we love has potential to be taken away (or is being taken away), we begin to see what is really important.

My diagnosis is not unique, though for some, my outcome may have been. I have met those who have defeated the vile curse of cancer and those who have been defeated by it. But whether it is cancer, catastrophe, or unexpected circumstance that seeks to take a life—I have met those who choose to leave a legacy, a hope, or a message behind regardless of their own victory or loss.

During my crisis I had to question whether I really want to live by what I had spent so many years professing—how great is the love God has for us. Did I really believe it?

How can cancer be love?

Maybe God loves others, but obviously I've done something wrong. Job loss, family separation, selling possessions to pay bills, and now cancer? This is the last straw.

I really wanted to hold onto my faith, but I needed help. And that help came in two very unexpected ways: social media and having to write a good-bye letter to my children.

Pray this:

God, I believe You have the power to heal and the power to withhold. I also believe You have the wisdom to know why. I know in heaven, where all things are made right, there is no illness or suffering and there is total peace as well. So I'm asking for heaven to come to earth in a tangible way. One way or another, will You make things right in this body of mine? Bring healing, bring total peace, or bring them both. I need them and I need You now.

Ponder this:

Don't worry about anything; instead, pray about everything. Tell God what you need, and thank him for all he has done. Then you will experience God's peace, which exceeds anything we can understand. His peace will guard your hearts and minds as you live in Christ Jesus.

- Paul @Philippians 4:6-7 (NLT)

"If you want the peace that passes understanding, you have to give up your right to understand."

- **Bill Johnson**, Bethel Church pastor

Believe this:

As I walk through this crisis I understand there are things I can control and things I can't control. I will not spend excess mental, spiritual, and physical energy trying to change circumstances that are beyond my ability. I will, however, purposely and passionately, pursue the best possible outcome. I will not let disappointment, disease, or disorder determine my self-worth or sense of hope.

Chapter 12

A Letter No One Wants But Everyone Needs

Break in, God, and break up this fight;
if you love me at all, get me out of here.
I'm no good to you dead, am I?
I can't sing in your choir if I'm buried in some tomb!
I'm tired of all this—so tired.
- David @Psalm 6:4-6 (MSG)

As word trickled out via Facebook, Twitter and who knows what, Cindy and I were overwhelmed with the love and support of so many people. Checks came in the mail, encouraging notes came over the net, and calls/texts popped up on my cell phone. Each like a tiny message from God, reminding me we reap what we sow in life.

Honestly, knowing people cared meant a lot to me, but the unexpected result was also a keen awareness that others were watching how I would walk through this newest crisis. And though some days I just wanted to cash in my chips, curse God, and die—the deepest part of me has always wanted to finish well.

And though none of us have control over when the actual finish is, we do have control over whether it will be "well," "mediocre," or "bitter." I don't want to be known as a guy who just finished mediocre or even bitter, do you?

An easy, breezy life can facilitate cruising toward finishing well, but for some reason it doesn't seem as earned as a person who has to struggle to get there. So as I read those texts and was buoyed by the emails, I also realized that whatever the outcome of this cancer thing, people would remember me for what I did, not what I had.

I don't know what your crisis is – but there are eyes upon you. It could be your kids, it could be your co-workers, it could be just a friend or two. Just keep in mind the life you lead isn't just about you. It is about them as well. What will the legacy be that you leave behind? Sure when it's all said and done, some will justify your bitter attitude due to a bitter circumstance, but why not choose to be one of those that rises above the path of least resistance towards influence and hope?

Maybe the name Bethany Hamilton rings a bell. On October 31, 2003, at the age of 13, a tiger shark attacked this promising young woman while she was surfing off the coast of Kauai's North Shore. She lost over 60 percent of her blood and her right arm was severed just inches below her shoulder. It was her faith in God, some quick thinking from her peers, and countless letters of encouragement from kids around the world that propelled her from choosing mediocrity toward building a legacy.

Now I don't know Bethany personally, and I hope to meet her someday, but what amazes me is she was back in the water surfing one month later! What? Okay, I saw the movie *Jaws* (I, II, & III) as a kid and have been sufficiently freaked out since then merely diving into the deep end of public pools, let alone submitting myself to the waves off the coast of anywhere. This woman is different… fear had opportunity in her life, but she gave it no power.

Embarrassment sought influence in her life, but she gave it no place. Disability provided excuses for her, but perseverance trumped adversity. Instead of downgrading to mediocrity, she chose legacy. And just over one year after such horrid circumstances tried to steal her life, she took first place in the Explorer Women's division of the 2005 NSSA National Championships – winning her first National Title.[15]

So from a broader perspective, social media and friendships had a major influence on my attitude and choices during my cancer crisis. God was showing me via my colon that finishing well is and will always be a choice. And even when everything seems to be about me, it really isn't just about me. But that truth became even more solidified when I decided to write a goodbye letter to the three most important people in my life: my daughter, Dakota; my son, Carter; and my soul-mate and wife, Cindy.

Why is it that when life seems the harshest, we re-evaluate what's really important to us? For some people I've met, that reevaluation comes too late. It's too late to reconcile what has been damaged, or too late to create memories that will be positive, or too late to build much of a legacy to remember. Still I've realized it is never *too late* to do something. Even the smallest gestures done in life, if given time to grow, can yield eternal consequences in someone else's life.

While I wrestled through the "what ifs" and "how comes" of my diagnosis one frustration kept surfacing in my heart: "*God, I'm not done yet. Especially with my family. I need more time! Please!*"

Those inner dialogues with God and myself forced me to ponder what actually I wasn't done with. I realized that I wanted to have a life-long influence on both of my kids' lives towards God and good. Suddenly, I felt like I may be out of time. So through a flood of tears I wrote each of my children a goodbye letter.

> Son,
>
> The fact that you are reading this means the unexpected and unwanted has happened – yet it was not unknown or unfelt by God. He is still present, still caring, and still loving, even when we don't understand.
>
> Now your journey changes. I have truly been sooo thankful to be your father – to be a part of helping you become such an incredible young man. Times will be tough, challenges will come, but always remember this word: CHOICE.
>
> You have the power to choose to continue

to grow to be a man of honor, a man of purpose, and a man of God. This is partly the legacy I have dreamed of leaving you, but only partly, because I believe there are important things about your life yet to be revealed. I believe in you, Son.

I know you will miss me. But if you listen… if you ask… you will always be able to hear my voice of confidence and wisdom inside of you. Why? Because you were created in my image – you and I are, and always will be, connected as father and son.

Do your best. When you make mistakes, pick yourself up and try again.

Honor and take care of Mom and Sister, trust God and care/stand-up for the poor and broken. These things will keep you on track and help you become the man you were created to be. (Galatians 6:1-5 MSG).

I love you, Son… I'll be waiting for you on the other side.

Love, Dad

Dakota Jasmine,

There has never been a moment that those two words that make up your name didn't bring some measure of joy to my soul. That's because from the very beginning you have been a treasure to me… a true gift from God.

So many times when you were just a little princess sitting on my lap I imagined what an amazing woman you would grow up to be. Now I see the young woman before me who was once just a little girl. I am so proud, so thankful, so blessed.

I may not be physically present with you from these days onward, but my love, my voice, my care can embrace you anytime you need me to.

Continue to grow in your faith, because these days will test it more than any. Faith is not for the easy times in our lives, but for times such as these.

On my side, it all makes sense now — I just grieve that you must try to figure it out without me holding your hand along the way.

Continue to care for others who have need, continue to be a friend to all, continue to love and help your mother and brother, continue to be "medicine dove" and my sunflower all your days — for that is what you were created to be.

I love you and am waiting for you on the other side.

Love, your Dad… your lion…

Geez... tears fill my eyes even as I copy these letters from my journal to this page today. I'm so glad my friends here at Jives Coffee know me well...

Here's my point.

Why do we have to wait till we are dying before we tell the people we love how much we care?

Why do such words of belief and encouragement only find their way out during times of desperation?

These are the things I want my kids to be living towards now. These are the things I want to be instilling into their lives a little dose at a time and not just as a last ditch effort in the end.

Who would you write such a letter to?

Who *should* you write such a letter to?

What's keeping you?

I tried so many times during my cancer crisis to write a similar letter to my wife... so many times I started and could only weep. Today, still, there is no such letter in my journal for her. There is a tremendous love in my heart. So much so I think I need to go tell her and not let my sentimentality turn to apathy, instead of action.

Try as we might to extend it with supplements, yoga and yogurt, life makes no promises regarding when it will end. We only get to choose if we will finish well or not. Thankfully, my cancer was treated with surgery and lots of weeks of recuperation. I had no need for chemotherapy, and my one-year check-up was clean.

Perhaps like you, I will live with the constant reminder of what happened and the subtle worry of whether it will return. However, I refuse to let worry dictate my life. *Worry is simply placing faith in the worst possible outcome, while hope is placing faith in the best.* Either way we exercise faith. Why not exercise it toward the good?

Whether it's my friend, Karen, who lost her battle with the brain tumor but continued to speak life and faith to others right up to the end, or whether it's Bethany, who overcame adversity and continues to build a legacy, or whether it's you and I, who continue to face challenges and disappointment… it all comes down to choice.

How do we choose to finish?

I don't want to live in denial — pretending the struggle, hurt, and fear are not present. I want to live in reality where I choose to give more power to hope than fear, more time to encouragement than whining, and more perseverance toward purpose than mediocrity. The story we receive is less important than the story we leave.

Pray this:

A prayer for healing
Hear my prayer, O Lord, heed my plea for mercy.
In time of trouble I call You, for You will answer me.
When pain and illness are my companions, let there be room in my heart for strength.
When the days and nights are filled with darkness, let the light of

courage find its place.
Help me endure the suffering and dissolve the fear; renew within
me the calm spirit of trust and peace.
Baruch Atah Adonai, Ro-fei HaCholim[16]
We praise you, O God, Healer of the Sick

Ponder this:

"Uncompromising trust in the love of God inspires us to thank God for the spiritual darkness that envelops us, for the loss of income, for the nagging arthritis that is so painful, and to pray from the heart, 'Abba, into our hands I entrust my body, mind, and spirit and this entire day – morning, afternoon, evening, and night.

Whatever you want of me, I want of me, falling into you and trusting in you in the midst of my life. Into your heart I entrust my heart, feeble, distracted, insecure, uncertain.

Abba, unto you I abandon myself in Jesus for an unanswered prayer, to give thanks in a state of inner desolation, to trust in the love of God in the face of the marvels, cruel circumstances, obscenities, and commonplaces of life is to whisper a doxology in darkness.'"

— **Brennan Manning**, author of *Ruthless Trust*

"This is not a letter but my arms around you for a brief moment."

- **Katherine Mansfield**
(New Zealander Writer, 1888-1923)

Believe this:

I don't know where this illness or crisis will take me. I may overcome, I may be overcome. Much of the outcome I cannot control, though I will try my best. What I can control is how I finish this journey, regardless of when that finish occurs.

So today, even in my crisis, I will find ways to finish well. I will find a way to leave a legacy that is worthy of the life I have been given, believing that even small gestures at this point may yield eternal significance for others later. I know now that how I begin a race is not as significant as how I choose to finish it. I will finish well.

Chapter 13

When You're Going Through Hell, Don't Stop!

God, God...my God!
Why did you dump me miles from nowhere?
Doubled up with pain, I call to God
all the day long. No answer. Nothing.
I keep at it all night, tossing and turning.

And here I am, a nothing—an earthworm,
something to step on, to squash.
Everyone pokes fun at me;
they make faces at me, they shake their heads:
"Let's see how God handles this one;
since God likes him so much, let him help him!".
- David @Psalm 22:1-2,6-8 (MSG)

Country singer, Rodney Atkins, released an interesting song during my season of suck. It is titled, "If You Are Going Through Hell" and if you'll read these lyrics with a bit of country twang they may resonate with you as well:

Well you know those times
When you feel like there's a sign there on your back
Says I don't mind if ya kick me

Seems like everybody has
Things go from bad to worse
You'd think they can't get worse than that
And then they do…

If you're going through hell
Keep on going, don't slow down
If you're scared, don't show it
You might get out
Before the devil even knows you're there…

Yep, pardner, my life has felt like a country song for the past three years. But even in the midst of the devil's kickin' us when we were down, God has continued to find a way to pick us back up (at least to our knees) so we can crawl forward and push through to another day.

Those offers of support… those rays of hope have come sometimes through friends, sometimes through prayer, and sometimes through a country song on the radio. But regardless of who or what has been doing the giving, I'm learning that I have to be positioning myself to do some receiving.

Listen, my friend, I'm writing this book from a place of struggling to survive, not from the "other side" where everything is viewed with rose-colored glasses and my life is filled with syrupy "Hallelujahs and Praise Gods."

No, I'm still at the place where to say "Hallelujah or Praise God" is an act of my will and God's worth. It isn't coming out of overflow like it used to; it is coming out of obedience like it must do.

I'm in marriage counseling to be sure that the stress of the years doesn't do irreparable damage to the most important relationship in my life. I'm finding my stack of job rejection letters is now growing larger than my stack of application cover letters. I'm watching what used to be life savings dwindle to weekly bills. I'm pushing through, but I haven't arrived yet.

But if you could tear open my soul and look inside, I truly believe that you would find a man who still has faith in God's goodness, and belief of a positive redemption of my life story. Why?

For two reasons: 1) I have witnessed it in too many other people's lives to not believe it could happen in mine. 2) I choose to continue to position myself to be ready for my own dramatic burning bush or slow creaking open door.

More important than *why* may actually be the *how*. Let's conclude our conversation in this book (though I pray it continues over coffee together sometime) by highlighting some ways that struggle is not yielding as much cowardness as it is courage in my life. Really, it is wisdom I've gathered during times of health that now mean more than ever as I find myself passing through hell, hoping the devil doesn't even notice I'm here.

Wait Aggressively

Years ago my friend, Marty Schaffer, taught me a phrase that continues to echo around in the somewhat hollow chambers of my soul: *wait aggressively.*

During times of indecision, unknowing and unwanted circumstances, continue to do everything you still know to do at this time and place in your life.

Some things are just obvious when it comes to being a follower of Christ: Honor your marriage vows, love and invest in your kids, read your Bible.

Other things are equally important: Feed the poor, care for the sick, build up the body of Christ, stand against injustice … you get the idea.

Waiting aggressively means not walking away from responsibilities, but purposing to keep in harmony with the will and Word of God.

You may feel like you are wandering perpetually in the land of despair, debt or disillusionment, but that is no excuse for not being present. Sometimes our hurt and pain turn our eyes so inward that we completely lose the outward focus our lives are intended to have. So until you hear, recognize, or know God is saying something different, go with what you know to be true.

But there is balance here. Don't go "ought-to-matic" either. *I ought to do this; I ought to do that. . .*

I once knew a woman who functioned this way. She was so busy doing good things for her church, that she was only serving her children halfway. The voices in her head said she ought to be at the women's Bible study, although her daughter wanted her to be a classroom aid. The voices in her head said she ought to practice with the worship team, although her kids wanted her help with their homework. The voices in her head said she ought to live in a nicer house and keep her full-time job so they could afford the nice home, although her heart said she needed to be home with her kids after school. This woman couldn't clearly hear God because she was focusing on all she "ought to" do.

So she took some time to question everything and wait aggressively. She went back to what was most important to her — pursuing the presence of God in her life. She cried out, "God, You are what I wanted from the very beginning. Pull my life back into the story You have for me."

That decision led her to follow the heart that God gave her, not the heart Wal-Mart offered her. It was then that she came alive in her calling to be a neighborhood mom. She not only made herself available to her own kids, but she also was available for her kids' friends as well. She found herself in the right place at the right time — at home with her children.

So, don't listen to your "ought to's" to find your purpose and hope. Instead, submit every "yes" and "no," every "ought to" and "should," to Jesus the Master, not just Fred the pastor.

As you push through this crisis, God may just be saying, "Tend to the struggle at hand, and let the other stuff wait," or he may be saying, "Get your eyes off yourself for awhile and onto others," I don't know.

What I do know is:

> • Waiting aggressively is not passivity, but purpose.

> • Waiting aggressively is not ignoring responsibility, but taking it.

> • Waiting aggressively is believing this season of struggle will end, and I will have my soul, body, and mind ready for what's next when it does.

Read the Bible from a Tribal Perspective

During my season of unraveling, my friends Dr. Suuqi-ina (Sue-key-na) and Qaumaniq (Kwaw-ma-neek) have offered perspective like few others. They haven't tried to plaster my life with Bible verses, though they know the Bible better than anyone I've met. They have offered perspective — oddly, in a sternly compassionate way. In a way that left me questioning many things about my assumptions about God and life, yet feeling more secure in them at the same time.

Dr. Suuqiina (his doctorate is in theology) is a native Inuit from Alaska. When he was growing up, our government took hundreds of Inuit children and "adopted" them into Anglo homes in order to train them to be culturally acceptable and fit a preconceived idea of what an "American" ought to be.

Suuqiina was one of those children torn from his brother and family and raised in an Anglo Christian home. There he was taught that God made a mistake when he made natives and that his former language and traditions where at best irrelevant and at worst demonic. The goal was to get him to speak the "right" language, use the "right" manners, and honor the "right" traditions. Over the years he was forced to grow in unnatural ways and learn to be someone he inherently knew he wasn't, a proper white European Christian boy.

Thankfully, Jesus has the power to redeem all things, including culture, and today Dr. Suuqiina and his Cherokee wife, Qaumaniq, travel the world helping people learn to worship the Creator Jesus in ways that are culturally natural to them and uncompromising biblical. They work tirelessly, untangling the web of cultural restrictions that have been placed on many oppressed people groups.

But for me, they helped untangle some of the confusion between my fairly sanitized 25-year version of Christianity which seems to subtly promise if I'll just drink a certain chicken soup for my soul, live life with a driven purpose, and sow the right amount of dollars to right ministries, I'm virtually assured to live my best life now. I'm bummed, because this ISN'T MY BEST LIFE NOW. It is only my life now and as soon as I can change it, I will.

Suuqiina offered some interesting insight to me one evening as we shared a meal together.

"Eric, perhaps you should try reading the Bible from a tribal perspective instead of an upper middle-class suburban white one. Your perspective is full of love, promise, and an entitlement mentality. It is *some of that* but more."

He was right. Much of what we see in life depends upon what we are looking for. I've spent a lot of years looking for provision and promise (which is there), but have failed to embrace struggle and turmoil in the midst of it.

The Bible is a story, a great narrative, of how God takes a small tribe of people and pulls them into the future He has for them. It is the story of a tribe of people, initially the Hebrews, and later a tribe called the "church," who are constantly under threat of extinction and persecution.

- Joseph is thrown into a well and left to die, then later falsely accused and put in prison... where's God's best there? (Joseph @Genesis 37)

- The Hebrews found themselves in and out of bondage and slavery, attacked from outside armies, and suffered betrayal from within over and over again.

- Moses lost his position of comfort and spent many years in exile in the desert... then wandered in another desert for 40 years... then didn't get to see the promised land ... (Moses @Exodus 2)

- Job was a man in good standing with God yet lost everything, and I mean everything — family, possessions, health ... Job @Job 2

- Many in the early church tribe were sold into slavery, sawed in two, stoned to death, forced to move ...

The point is that throughout God's story, there is an undercurrent of survival and struggle. It isn't just a book about being happy; it is a book about pressing on and pressing in. The story isn't always some candy coated, everything has a *High School Musical* outcome … but somehow, somewhere, God in His sovereignty and presence keeps the bigger story moving along. Some in the story get to see the "promise" while here on earth; some only get to pass on that promise to the next generation.

Still, throughout it all there are countless "suddenlies." Times when at the very last moment… when all hope seems lost… that God intervenes, rescues his people, or intrudes in such a way that hope is not lost nor his love fully hidden.

Honestly, sometimes I don't get it. Why a friend of mine can pray to find a great deal on running shoes at the store and get them, while others can pray for healing for the child's addiction and later sit at that same child's funeral brought on by an overdose.

It is humbling. It is frustrating. It is confusing.

But when I pull back and see the bigger story of God, when I take myself out of my microscopic moment into his macroscopic movement, I realize that most often God's intervention and presence occur as we position ourselves to receive. Not position ourselves to receive what we want or expect, but avail ourselves to receive what comes our way. Not with passivity, but purpose and faith. Not with denial or ignorance, but trust and perseverance.

Maybe holding those four ingredients together — purpose, faith, trust, and perseverance — I am ready to have some chicken soup for my weak soul and will learn that my attitude helps me live my best life now, regardless of what that life may look like.

Buffer Against Your Addictions and Bad Habits

We are a culture of anesthetizers. Seems every time we have an ache or pain, every time we have a negative experience from breaking up to bad hair, there is a product available to soothe us, numb us, and take the hurt away. A stroll through WalMart's medicine aisles convinced me that we live in a culture of anesthetizers.

As I slurp a double Americano to keep my headache at bay, let me tell you what I saw. Ten pain medicines said "maximum strength," and a few even had "new and improved maximum strength." What does that mean? Maximum strength — is that the most a human body can handle? If I took just a little bit extra, would my head explode or would I go into a coma? It seems everything for alleviating our pain is either maximum strength, longer lasting, new and improved, or fast acting.

Then I watch the alcohol commercials on television. All those pretty people — they seem so relaxed, so happy, so together. My life is a mess in comparison. The only difference is they have a drink in their hand. Okay, so they have jobs, definitely are better looking than me, and live in Utopia…

but it all comes back to the booze. Could the alcohol really make my life feel better?

Then there's the soothing comfort of food… from the food channel, countless restaurant advertisements, to the appeal of a mom's comfort as she bakes Nestle Toll House cookies. Food, food, glorious food!

Of course if my relationship is under stress, I can always find comfort in fantasizing about past relationships through social media connections or virtual satisfaction online.

If all else fails there is always a chemical somewhere readily available to boost me up, mellow me out, or help me escape to another world… even if just for an hour or two or 20.

I understand. As a culture we spend billions, both legally and illegally, treating the physical symptoms of pain and then double that again as we drink and crank away our emotional ones. Pain is bad, relief is good.

We have all learned ways to comfort ourselves when our body, heart, or mind is stressed. Often those methods of comfort serve a purpose for a time, but when they become *necessary* for relief and not just to *aid* relief we should pause and take note. When our chosen mode of relief is actually *life-stealing* and not *life-giving*, we should immediately reevaluate our decisions.

Listen, I'm not just talking about popping an Advil for minor aches, or eating a little chocolate for some comfort after a rough day. I'm talking about when certain substances begin to take away our sanity. When the stress of life begs us to turn to things our hearts know we should avoid, and our flesh feels compelled to receive. When the lack of chemical causes deeper aches, or the lack of a food stirs deeper pain.

Pain hurts. Disillusionment skews reality. Loss creates a vacuum that longs to be filled. These are legitimate needs that we often choose to meet in illegitimate ways. Whether we choose to anesthetize with porn, pot, or popcorn — it seems that deep pain or chronic stress seeks to wear out our self-will and persistently beg for an opportunity to "help us feel better." And when we give in, we can be the source of causing our own sky falling.

After so many years working with friends in recovery, this past couple years has shown me that even I, Dr. E…, Mr. Human Sexuality Professor…, author, teacher, and pretty good guy… is only ONE decision away from my own addictions and poor choices. One decision away from anesthetizing myself in a life-stealing way instead of a life-giving way.

During this time, I've had to beef up my internet filters, renew authentic accountability with men that I trust, and humbly be honest with my wife regarding weaknesses that I feel.

Never before has alcohol, porn, and escapism (movies, X-box, ESPN) been so appealing in my life. And my wife has her own demons that seek to pull her away from life-giving comfort towards life-stealing ones. Ironically, we are aware how they work against us as husband and wife, and for each other as demonic tools, in order to divide and conquer our marriage and family. We have to be honest about our own frailty and learn to walk in the opposite spirit.

Listen, it is not like the devil is looking at your life or mine and thinking, "Well, they've got a lot going on for now. I'll just hold back for awhile till they get things together."

NO! The enemy has a plan for your life and mine — a plan to destroy all the good that remains — to kick you while you are down, and then kick again. Falling back into unhealthy habits or addictions only greases the rails on that downward slide. So choose this day to not give up more ground. Buffer up your defenses and seek help if necessary. You can start your day or your week over at anytime. Just because it started bad, doesn't mean it has to finish that way.

During this season buffering my defenses I was convicted by these words of Oswald Chambers:

> "The first thing to do in examining the power that dominates me is to take hold of the unwelcome fact that I am responsible for being thus dominated. If I am a slave to myself, I am to blame because at a point away back I yielded to myself. Likewise, if I obey God I do so because I have yielded myself to Him.
>
> Yield in childhood to selfishness, and you will find it the most enchaining tyranny on earth. There is no power in the human soul of itself to break the bondage of a disposition

formed by yielding. Yield for one second to anything in the nature of lust (remember what lust is: "I must have it at once," whether it be the lust of the flesh or the lust of the mind) - once yield and though you may hate yourself for having yielded, you are a bondslave to that thing. There is no release in human power at all but only in the Redemption. You must yield yourself in utter humiliation to the only One who can break the dominating power viz., the Lord Jesus Christ - "He hath anointed me . . . to preach deliverance to all captives."

You find this out in the most ridiculously small ways - "Oh, I can give that habit up when I like." You cannot, you will find that the habit absolutely dominates you because you yielded to it willingly. It is easy to sing - "He will break every fetter" and at the same time be living a life of obvious slavery to yourself. Yielding to Jesus will break every form of slavery in any human life."

- **Oswald Chambers**, *My Utmost For His Highest*

The Relationship is More Important than the Issue

Marital research has shown that the two most influential factors that lead to divorce are financial stress and marital infidelity (whether virtual or actual). Interestingly, many marriage counselors will tell you that it is financial troubles and its subsequent tension within the marriage that often push a couple apart and towards "attractive alternatives."

Isn't it interesting how when there is stress and tension surrounding a marriage, small problems become huge issues within the marriage? Maybe it's just us, but Cindy and I have seen minor problems become major arguments ever since this season of unraveling. Our relationship has been tested like never before. Thankfully, we have held on because many years ago we adopted a philosophy towards marriage that can bear the weight of disillusionment and misunderstanding. Simply put, it is: *"The relationship is more important than the issue."*

During times of crisis, issues swirl around our lives like dirt devils in the Mojave, causing panicky decisions and blinding us to what's truly important. Whether you are in severe crisis or not, whether you are married or not, keeping in mind the relationship is more important than the issue, can save a lot of heartache later on.

Have you ever met someone who would rather be right than happy? Winning the argument, proving their point, or coming out on top just seems to be more of the goal than building or maintaining relationship? I'm not saying we should avoid tension or pretend differences don't exist. What is important is to keep our priorities straight. Every problem may have a beginning, middle, and end — but marriage and our relationship with God should be perpetual.

So during times of struggle and complaint, I have found things go much better if I start by deciding (yes, sometimes it is purely an act of my will) that I will not let this problem take precedence over my relationship.

There have been many times I've come to God with so much anger… so much frustration… so much complaint… that at first I had to choose to say, "Jesus, our friendship is more important than what is happening in my life right now, but I am angry. I don't want to lose you in the process of working this out…"

Come to think of it, there have been times Cindy has come to me or I have come to her with much the same attitude. We have had more disagreements on what to do next, how to approach the next decision, or how to handle a hurt between us than ever before. But the times we remind each other that we have a choice — "Either to have an old happy marriage, or an old unhappy marriage, but either way we are going to be married when this is over…" — our greatest sense of strength becomes evident: each other.

So during your times of frustration, be careful you are not sacrificing the relationships that are most important to you. Be careful you are not turning anger about circumstances toward the people you love and need. When all hell seems to be breaking loose around you, don't give the devil the opportunity to break things loose within you as well. There are times that it is more important to be happy than just to be right. There are times the relationship is more important than the issue.

Every Crisis has a Beginning, a Middle, and an End

If you've ever been to a track meet or watched the news highlights after a big race like the Boston Marathon, you'll notice the people who get all the attention are not the one's who started off well, but those that actually finish. Oftentimes we celebrate and highlight not the person who finished first, but the person who shouldn't have finished but did. They inspire us. Such a person who actually finishes takes on all new relevance when we learn about how difficult their start or mid-race was.

I tell people all the time in counseling, and now myself, "Every crisis has a beginning, middle, and end. It is the decisions we make at the beginning and middle that will determine if we create a new, but unnecessary, crisis for ourselves at the end." Even if crises seem to compound upon our lives, they can be looked at as separate events.

The loss of our home during the 2008 economic collapse was a nightmare that seemed it would never end. The event itself peppered our lives with all sorts of tangential issues (loss of income, embarrassment, having to move, etc). But what felt like a never-ending problem did finally have an end. It may not have been the end we wanted or dreamed of, but nonetheless it did end.

Because we tried to walk with integrity, made the best decisions we could during chaos, and let go of what we ultimately could not hold… when the house finally short-sold and the bogus court proceedings ended — we were done. The scar may remain, but the injury doesn't have to control our future anymore.

I've met others in similar situations, who vandalized their house before moving out, tore out ALL the copper pipes and wiring to resell it, and ripped up carpets, etc. in order to make a statement to the bank. I understand the anger and resentment behind such decisions, oh do I, but such actions only created new problems for them later.

Here is some decision-making advice that helped me during all these times of compounding stink in my life — try to evaluate each decision in three ways:

> 1. Will this decision likely create a new and unnecessary problem/crisis for me later? If so, is the new problem worth what the current decision is solving?
>
> 2. How will this current decision shape the middle of this current crisis and the foreseeable end?
>
> 3. How will this decision line up with how I profess to believe and behave as a person? What is the legacy I am leaving?

I know it is hard to believe sometimes, but *every* crisis does have an end. Only God knows what that end will look like. But as I pray for the light at the end of my dark days, I pray for you as well. Don't give up hope … at the very least don't give up looking for hope. It is out there as assuredly as the darkness. Together we will push through tough times to find the promise on the other side.

Have you ever pondered why Jesus was born in a stable, in the dark of night, in a town nobody cared about? It may not have just been about cuddly sheep and cute children's ministry Christmas plays. He may have been making a much more profound statement to the world, and more specifically, to you and me.

God's life is often birthed in the darkest places of our lives. I pray we both find the reality of that promise soon … Peace to you, my friend, as you wrestle your way toward hope.

Pray this:

My Lord God, I have no idea where I am going.
I do not see the road ahead of me.
I cannot know for certain where it will end.

Nor do I really know myself, and the fact that I think that I am following your will does not mean that I am actually doing so. But I believe that the desire to please you does in fact please you.
And I hope I have that desire in all that I am doing.
I hope that I will never do anything apart from that desire.
And I know that if I do this you will lead me by the right road though I may know nothing about it.

Therefore will I trust you always though I may seem to be lost and in the shadow of death.

I will not fear, for you are ever with me, and you will never leave me to face my perils alone.
—**Thomas Merton**[17]

Ponder this:

I know God will not give me anything I can't handle. I just wish that He didn't trust me so much.

— **Mother Teresa**

I have prayed for you, that your faith not fail. And after you have come through your time of testing, turn to your companions and give them a fresh start.

— **Jesus @Luke 22:32, MSG**

"Let me tell you something you already know. The world ain't all sunshine and rainbows. It is a very mean and nasty place and it will beat you to your knees and keep you there permanently if you let it. You, me, or nobody is gonna hit as hard as life. But it ain't how hard you hit; it's about how hard you can get hit, and keep moving forward. How much you can take, and keep moving forward. That's how winning is done. Now, if you know what you're worth, then go out and get what you're worth. But you gotta be willing to take the hit, and not pointing fingers saying you ain't where you are because of him, or her, or anybody. Cowards do that and that ain't you. You're better than that!"

— **Rocky Balboa**

Believe this:

Though circumstances in my life are trying to make me feel disillusioned, indebt and discouraged, I have this ray of hope: even this crisis will have an end. Though problems may feel overwhelming and insurmountable, I have this ray of hope: I do not have to walk alone, for God is with me whether I feel him or not.

Though I don't know what is next in my life, I have this ray of hope: I can choose to wait aggressively and position my life for the best possible outcome. Regardless of how I began this race, or struggled in the middle, I choose to finish well.

Chapter 14

Suddenly ...

It's always been one of my favorite words in the Bible: *suddenly.* But through this two years of suck in my life, suddenly felt so far away. Nonetheless, I often found myself hoping for a "suddenly," because "suddenly" has occurred in the past for so many others. Somehow I knew that if I wrote this book after my "suddenly" happened, it would taint the visceral nature of what I was going through in the present. So there is an eight-month gap between chapter 13 and chapter 14 of this book. Eight more months of waiting, wondering, and wanting... then *suddenly* things changed.

It happened when the church Cindy and I were attending *suddenly* needed a part-time staff counselor, the university I was teaching part-time for *suddenly* wanted to put me on long-term contract... and then *suddenly* a part-time counselor wasn't enough — my church needed a full-time recovery ministry and teaching pastor. *Suddenly* the home my wife knew we could never afford to buy opened up for rent at a price my new salary could afford. *Suddenly* I was preaching again, caring for the broken, and finding myself back in the ministry saddle. After nearly three years of longing and pain, *suddenly* within a four-week period provision, purpose, and people where back in our lives again! Geez...

that's bizarre…

However, my suddenly may or may not be like your suddenly. God has your suddenly in mind. It is there, my friend. It has to happen because God has written your storyline. The choices we make can either detour us from the story or allow God to bring it to pass in His way and timing. I'm on the backside of my latest crisis. In the immortal words of my iPhone ringtone by Jimmy Buffet, "I can see clearly now the rain has gone…"

Great. I get it. My suddenly doesn't change your need for one. However, I do hope it inspires you to believe for one. Just don't miss it because suddenlies come in various forms:

Suddenly: God allows us to see ourselves….

How many of us have had God suddenly turn on the light in our life?

Suddenly we see things for the way they really are, not what we are pretending them to be. Suddenly we see ourselves for *who* we really are, not what we are pretending to be. Some call it hitting bottom… admitting your powerlessness… taking off the mask… realizing that you have been living your own story and not God's.

I spoke in a high school class one time as a guest for world religions week. I got to be the token evangelical Christian representative out of a week of guest speakers from Hindu, Islam, Mormon, and Buddhist presentations. I was doing my best to be a cool and relevant representation of the Jesus I thought these students needed to hear about. But one young man in particular was starting to really chap my hide. He was especially contentious, challenging everything I said and mocking my beliefs. I think the teacher was enjoying wondering whether I was going to release my own version of a holy jihad upon him at some point.

Then he asked the standard question, "So if your God is love and so looovvinnggg (snicker, snicker), why would He send someone like me to hell?"

I responded, "Because He loves you. Listen, what if you so conditioned your entire life, your living, breathing, waking, and sleeping moments to not want God involved? What if, by your words today and every day, you made it clear you wanted no part of God's presence in your life? Wouldn't it be the absolute meanest thing He could do to *force* you to spend eternity with Him. He loves you enough to let you go to hell."

Suddenly, the light came on in this young man's soul. He literally went pale from fear and conviction. Suddenly, he saw himself for who he really was and not who he was pretending to be. His antagonist attitude toward faith was actually bringing him closer and closer to a confrontation with the God he didn't believe in. Not unlike a man named Saul in the Bible who spent his first number of years persecuting the church and the later years dying for it.

"...so that if he found any there who belonged to the Way, whether men or women, he might take them as prisoners to Jerusalem. As he neared Damascus on his journey, suddenly a light from heaven flashed around him. He fell to the ground and heard a voice say to him, "Saul, Saul, why do you persecute me?"

- Luke @Acts 9:2-4 (TNIV)

Paul got knocked off his high horse and invited into a whole new reality. How about you today? Are there areas in your life where you are pretending to be something you ultimately don't want to be? Are there people in your life who seem so far from knowing God that you've given up hope? There may be a suddenly about to happen that changes everything.

Suddenly: God empowers your mission…

Ever just find yourself waiting? Waiting for a purpose… waiting for direction… waiting for answers… Earlier in this book I introduced you to a phrase: Wait Aggressively. That means we need to wait until we have clear direction in our lives regarding the next step. But we don't do it passively. We do everything we are supposed to be doing in the present. Sometimes that means going back to the last thing you heard God telling you to do but have let slip away. Sometimes that means just be obedient to the obvious while waiting for the obscure.

Believe God will answer you, because sometimes God reveals His mission to you suddenly…

> "At Caesarea there was a man named Cornelius, a centurion in what was known as the Italian Regiment. He and all his family were devout and God-fearing; he gave generously to those in need and prayed to God regularly. One day at about three in the afternoon he had a vision. He distinctly saw an angel of God, who came to him and said, "Cornelius!"
>
> Cornelius stared at him in fear. "What is it, Lord?" he asked.
>
> The angel answered, "Your prayers and gifts to the poor have come up as a memorial offering before God. Now send men to Joppa to bring back a man named Simon who is called Peter. He is staying with Simon the tanner, whose house is by the sea."
>
> When the angel who spoke to him had gone, Cornelius called two of his servants and a devout soldier who was one of his attendants. He told them everything that had happened and sent them to Joppa."

- **Luke @Acts 10:1-8 (TNIV)**

This is a great example of a normal guy waiting aggressively. He had no idea that someday *his story* would be part of the greatest story ever! What caught my attention in this passage recently was how Cornelius' prayers and gifts to the poor had come before God. Cornelius' obedience to doing the things he knew he should be doing caught God's attention! Then, suddenly, God empowered his mission and life to something that would help change the course of church history. God used Cornelius to tutor Peter, one of the great pillars of the early church!

Listen, if you are waiting for direction and purpose in your life, wait aggressively… your suddenly will come.

Suddenly: God empowers your courage…

I remember being baptized as a follower of Christ back when I was 16. I was part of a new church start that met in a middle school cafeteria on Sundays. My pastor had to borrow a baptismal from another church so a number of us could get dunked one Saturday night. My pastor wanted each "dunkee" to have a life verse from the Bible that God would sear into their hearts during baptism. I choose Romans 1:16, "For I am not ashamed of the gospel of Christ, for it is the power of God that brings salvation to anyone who believes."

What my pastor neglected to tell me was that such verses are often tested in our lives in order to be proven true. Geez, sometimes I wish I would have chosen one on wealth and prosperity. Over the years I've had countless opportunities to either cower down or stand up for what I believe.

How 'bout for you? How much fortitude does your faith have under pressure?

Where is your faith challenged the most — at work… school… home… the mall… in private in front of your computer screen?

If you ever feel a lack of courage in your walk with Christ, take heart! This passage is for you! We pick up the story after Peter and John are arrested for preaching the Gospel and doing good deeds. They are threatened and told no longer to share the good news of Christ. Gathering together with other Christ followers they pray:

> "'Now, Lord, consider their threats and enable your servants to speak your word with great boldness. Stretch out your hand to heal and perform miraculous signs and wonders through the name of your holy servant Jesus.'
>
> After they prayed, the place where they were meeting was shaken. And they were all filled with the Holy Spirit and spoke the word of God boldly."
>
> - Luke @Acts 4:29-31 (TNIV)

What makes this passage significant is that these early Christians were not praying for relief from oppression or circumstances, but courage and boldness. Maybe some of us are praying for the wrong "suddenly" in our lives. We want relief from the pressure or persecution. We want the fruit of helping others know Christ without the risk. Often where we want relief, God wants obedience!

Suddenly: God sets you free from bondage...

Have you ever felt trapped? Absolutely powerless to get out of your current situation or circumstances? It could be trapped chemically, where the chains of addiction have wrapped themselves so tight around you that even if you wanted to walk away you couldn't.

How about being trapped in success? Perhaps you have this burning desire to make a change but can't because responsibility, status and mortgage payments feel more like anchors than safety nets.

What about being trapped in a lifeless marriage... financial debt... emotional pain... memory from your past? There are seasons in our lives, sometimes by what we do and sometimes by what is done to us, that leave us feeling imprisoned and helpless. Oh, have I got a suddenly for you!

> "The night before Herod was to bring him to trial, Peter was sleeping between two soldiers, bound with two chains, and sentries stood guard at the entrance. Suddenly an angel of the Lord appeared and a light shone in the

cell. He struck Peter on the side and woke him up. "Quick, get up!" he said, and the chains fell off Peter's wrists.

Then the angel said to him, "Put on your clothes and sandals." And Peter did so. "Wrap your cloak around you and follow me," the angel told him."

- Luke @Acts 12:6-8 (TNIV)

The backstory of this passage is prayer. People were praying intensely for Peter. Other contexts would lead us to believe Peter himself was probably praying and worshiping until he fell asleep. Then suddenly!

God may be showing some of you the way out of your bondage and pain today. He has even kicked a few of you in the side and said get up. But you have to be the one to get up! You have to be willing to follow his plan. He can break off any chains that are holding you back, but He still requires us to get up and get moving. This is God's promise. Even when there seems to be no way out — suddenly.

That's what I love about recovery ministries. Sometimes I see people dramatically set free, like *shazaam!...* then everything's better. Other times I see people learn to struggle out their freedom over the course of years and sometimes decades. But freedom is freedom and I'll take it any way I can get it!

Suddenly: We realize God's been there all along...

This is a book about when the sky is falling. Because sometimes is does. We could look at example after example in the Bible of how God suddenly intervenes and made-for-Hollywood level miracles occur. Those are the ones that lift us up and give us hope. Those are the ones that serve as little lamp posts along a path that seems to have grown dark.

But there is another suddenly that is harder to grasp. A suddenly that I have yet to experience, yet believe with every fiber of my being exists. It is a suddenly that every culture, every tribe, ever person seems to encounter. It is a suddenly that seems so conclusive and yet is so open ended. A suddenly that inevitability overwhelms some and gives hope to many.

You see, all those people being miraculously healed in the Bible ended up no different than those who are never mentioned or those whose lives were taken by murder and martyrdom. Death overtakes us all. We are born into this flesh propelled toward that inevitable closure. Then there is the other side. In my role as a pastor, a fire-department chaplain, and as a human being, I have been around this death thing more than most. Sometimes its face is horrific as it steals life through tragedy and disease, while other times it masks itself as beauty as a person passes quietly in their sleep. Until Christ comes, Death is inevitable—but not it's sting.

However this life ends, through pain and struggle or pleasurable purpose, there is a suddenly on the other side. Suddenly, we will see the face of God. Suddenly, all this tragedy will make sense. Suddenly, the times of struggle that you felt were never going to end become like a blink in the eye, in light of the eternity that awaits.

If these past years of suck in my life have taught me anything... If facing the fear of loss of my life, my possessions and even my faith have taught me something valuable it is this: Both fear and hope are choices I get to make — whether my sky is falling or my crops are growing. Fear is faith in the worst possible outcome and hope is faith that there is a "suddenly" still waiting for me...

Pray this:

The Serenity Prayer
God grant me the serenity
to accept the things I cannot change;
courage to change the things I can;
and wisdom to know the difference.

Living one day at a time;
Enjoying one moment at a time;
Accepting hardships as the pathway to peace;
Taking, as He did, this sinful world
as it is, not as I would have it;
Trusting that He will make all things right
if I surrender to His Will;
That I may be reasonably happy in this life
and supremely happy with Him
Forever in the next.
Amen.
— **Reinhold Niebuhr**

Ponder this:

"If patience is worth anything, it must endure to the end of time. And a living faith will last in the midst of the blackest storm."

—Mahatma Gandhi

"Each one of these people of faith died not yet having in hand what was promised, but still believing. How did they do it? They saw it way off in the distance, waved their greeting, and accepted the fact that they were transients in this world. People who live this way make it plain that they are looking for their true home. If they were homesick for the old country, they could have gone back any time they wanted. But they were after a far better country than that — heaven country. You can see why God is so proud of them, and has a City waiting for them."

- @Hebrews 11:13-16, MSG

Believe this:

I admit I really don't know how this is all going to end, but I know it will. I choose to let hope guide me instead of having fear drive me. I choose to believe that there is a "suddenly" awaiting me and whether on this side or the other, there will come a day when it all makes sense, when I will see my story in light of God's bigger story. May I go out singing...

"My Hope is Built on Nothing Less"

by Edward Mote, 1797-1874

1. My hope is built on nothing less
Than Jesus' blood and righteousness;
I dare not trust the sweetest frame,
But wholly lean on Jesus' name.
On Christ, the solid Rock, I stand;
All other ground is sinking sand.

2. When darkness veils His lovely face,
I rest on His unchanging grace;
In every high and stormy gale
My anchor holds within the veil.
On Christ, the solid Rock, I stand;
All other ground is sinking sand.

3. His oath, His covenant, and blood
Support me in the whelming flood;
When every earthly prop gives way,
He then is all my Hope and Stay.
On Christ, the solid Rock, I stand;
All other ground is sinking sand.

4. When He shall come with trumpet sound,
Oh, may I then in Him be found,
Clothed in His righteousness alone,
Faultless to stand before the throne!
On Christ, the solid Rock, I stand;
All other ground is sinking sand.

Eric & Cindy's Calendar of Crisis

(Better an appendix than my colon…)

Though my story isn't as significant as your story, I wanted to provide a chronology of events for those of you who like to keep life a little more orderly. I regularly meet people whose personal journey is even more heartbreaking or stressful than ours. So don't read this chronology as a plea for pity, but as a statement of empathy. I understand — sometimes life is harsh… our choice it to press on, press in, and push through, even when it seems the sky is falling.

June 2006

Moved from Port Angeles, WA to Southern California to become teaching/recovery pastor of a 4000-member church.

Eric feels he is in his dream job and our friendships grow deep over that initial year and a half period.

January 2008

Three church staff members laid off, a 5% pay cut for Eric, and Cindy's hours cut in half.

Eric offered to resign and work at the college so the others wouldn't have to be laid off but was told his role was needed.

Began trying to contact bank to modify our home loan.

March 2008

Taxes on our house went up $500/month and we couldn't make payments anymore... still trying to modify loan.

April 2008

Cindy had to quit at the church and work elsewhere to get more hours.

May 2008

Eric's grandmother passed away. Eric facilitates the service in Colorado.

September 2008

Bank won't work with us, so we decide to short sale our house.

November 2008

Eric offered a position as a senior pastor at another church but turned it down since we had made a 5-year commitment to our current church and felt his position was secure.

December 2008

Eric told that his position was something the church could no longer afford and would probably be laid off, thus he should start looking for another job.

January 2009

Contacted by church in Colorado to interview for a teaching pastor position.

February 2009

Officially given notice of his layoff, effective June 2009

One week later, the Colorado church informs Eric they could not hire him due to the economic instability it was now experiencing.

March 2009

Moved out of our home due to delays in short sale and threats of foreclosure. After moving out, the bank changed its mind and granted extended time. Now we had to take care of our old house, and pay for a rental while waiting for sale to go through (this process went on for 11 more months).

April 2009

Friends visiting from England were in a very serious car accident, hospitalizing three of them.

Decided our daughter should stay in California for her senior year. Some good friends graciously "adopted" her so she could stay.

With no other jobs opportunities in California, Eric decides to take a job with a friend in Las Vegas doing time-share sales. This would keep us close enough to drive to see our daughter in California.

May 2009

Cindy has major surgery.

Two weeks later, Eric rents a room in Las Vegas.

Cindy stays back to recuperate and for the kids to finish the school year.

June 2009

Moved our daughter in with her new "senior-year" family.

July 2009

The kids and Cindy went back to Washington, our first family vacation in two years, but Eric could no longer go.

Eric stays in Vegas and finds a suitable home for rent.

Upon returning to California and having only 10 days to pack, Cindy went to check on our old house. She found someone had broken through a window. She got it fixed and went back the next day to only to find it broken into again, but this time someone had completely smashed the sliding glass door and there was shattered glass everywhere — Cindy completely broke down. Friends helped clean it up.

Our friend, Kap, agrees to stay there until the sale went through (we were now on our second offer).

August 2009

Cindy and Carter move to Vegas to join Eric.

September 2009

The second offer didn't go through on our house and now we had a third offer.

We were supposed to receive the small deposit from the second offer but the buyers disputed it and filed a lawsuit against us.

November 2009

The family our daughter is living with loses their house, and she has to move to a new location with them.

Our house finally short-sold, but we were still being sued over the deposit.

Eric took the time-share sales job and becomes a week-to-week financial stressor due to low sales.

February 2010

Eric is diagnosed with colon cancer.

Ten days later Eric has major surgery to remove a one-foot section of his intestine.

March 2010

Celebrated Cindy's mom's 70th birthday with extended family in Arizona (her parents are from Colorado)

Ten days later, Cindy's dad has a heart attack.

Though still struggling from surgery, Cindy and Eric drive to Phoenix to see her dad. He dies 20 hours after our arrival.

April 2010

Still recuperating from surgery, Eric officiates Cindy's father's funeral in Colorado.

May 2010

Went to court over the deposit and won, but buyers appeal.

June 2010

Our daughter graduates from high school.

While trying to celebrate our daughter's graduation, we were also trying to take care of the ruling on the appeal. The court had lost our documents and it took several trips to the courthouse to work out issues. Finally, on the day of our daughter's graduation party, it was resolved.

July 4, 2010

Just prior to coming to our home for the 4th of July, our close friends' 15-month old son, Jude, falls in a pool.

We spent three days at the hospital while Jude was in a coma.

Eric walks our friends through the decision to turn off life support. Jude passed away in his parents arms on July 7, 2010.

August 2010

Eric flew to WA to help officiate Jude's funeral.

September 2010

Eric officially put on contract at work (if he didn't get a certain amount of sales by the end of the month he would be laid off).

A mega-church in the Midwest called to interview Eric for a position as a recovery ministry leader.

On the last day of the month Eric makes a sale that allowed him to keep his time-share job.

November 2010

Eric continues to interview with mega-church and is put on contract again for low sales.

After working during Thanksgiving week, Eric thought he made enough sales to keep his job but then one of his buyers canceled and he was officially laid off.

December 2010

Eric and Cindy flew out to mega-church for more

interviews and for us to meet with their real estate agent. We were trying to hold on, feeling confident Eric was going to get the recovery pastor job.

While Eric was speaking in Washington State, he received a call from mega-church and was informed they weren't going to hire him.

With no other options, Eric and Cindy give notice to their landlords and begin selling what they could and packing in order to move in with Eric's parents in Colorado.

Christmas Eve 2010 they arrive in Colorado broke, frustrated, and disillusioned.

January 2011

Only able to find part-time work teaching at a local university, Eric feels led to begin writing "The Sky is Falling."

January 2012

A month full of suddenlies… a full-time position at my church, an incredible home to rent within our budget, found an awesome deal on furniture off Craigslist…

End Notes

Chapter 2

[1] Sadly, Kristina's sister did pass away from complications associated with her condition, but Kristina and her mom continue to persevere, partly due to their faith in God and the loving way they serve others.

[2] Kristina's story inspired Sandy and me to launch BeyondTheInk.com.

[3] I found this prayer last year on a Catholic website. You don't have to be Catholic to pray this type of prayer, just someone who is suffering. http://www.catholic.org/prayers/prayer.php?p=873

Chapter 3

[4] Despite common misconception, Saint Patrick was not a native of Ireland, but of Scotland. When he was about sixteen he was captured by Irish raiders and taken as a slave to Ireland, where he lived for six years before escaping and returning to his family in Britain. Obeying the call of God, he later returned to Ireland as a missionary sharing the love of Christ with those who had once been his captors. By the eighth century he had become the patron saint of Ireland.

Chapter 4

[5] Author: John Birch Website:

http://www.faithandworship.com/healing_prayers_3.htm

I came across this website a few years ago while studying Celtic prayers. John puts words into prayers that seem so authentic and heartfelt. Pray it the same way.

[6] From God's Little Instruction Book for the Class of 2011, David C. Cook publishing, pg. 148 – I know that's odd, but I was flipping through it at a bookstore one day and this statement caught my attention.

[7] Viktor E. Frankl speaks from experience, not just theory. He suffered in at least three different concentration camps during Nazi rule. As a result of the suffering he saw and endured in these camps he came to his hallmark conclusion that even in the most absurd, dark and dehumanizing situations, life has potential meaning even in suffering.

Chapter 5

[8] Corrie ten Boom (Amsterdam, 1892 – Orange, California, April 15, 1983) was a Dutch Christian Holocaust survivor who helped many Jews escape the Nazis during World War II. In 1970, Corrie co-wrote her autobiography, The Hiding Place, released in 1971. Powerful story. Read it.

Chapter 6

[9] Actually this quote is often attributed to C.S. Lewis. Singer, Kenny Rogers, said you have to "know when to fold 'em." Carrie from Sex in the City said, "But maybe the best any of us can do is not quit, play the hand we've been dealt, and accessorize what we've got." And of course Jesus told us, "Give, and it shall be given to you. For whatever measure you deal out to others, it will be dealt to you in return." *Now that would make for an interesting poker game!*

[10] Choosing poorly during these moments doesn't necessarily mean the end. It just means consequences and a chance to grow again. David choose poorly with Bathsheba (2 Samuel 11) and Peter was restored even after blowing it by denying Jesus (John 21).

[11] The Valley of Vision: A Collection of Puritan Prayers & Devotions. Arthur Bennett ed. Written in the sixteenth and seventeenth centuries – republished in 1975.

Chapter 8

[12] Elisabeth's first husband, Jim Elliot, was killed in 1956 while attempting to make missionary contact with the Auca tribe of eastern Ecuador. She later spent two years as a missionary to the tribe

members who killed her husband. The movie, *The End of the Spear*, was released in 2006 and is a great retelling of the story.

Chapter 11

[13] Howlader N, Noone AM, Krapcho M, Neyman N, Aminou R, Waldron W, Altekruse SF, Kosary CL, Ruhl J, Tatalovich Z, Cho H, Mariotto A, Eisner MP, Lewis DR, Chen HS, Feuer EJ, Cronin KA, Edwards BK (eds). SEER Cancer Statistics Review, 1975-2008, National Cancer Institute. Bethesda, MD, http://seer.cancer.gov/csr/1975_2008/, based on November 2010 SEER data submission, posted to the SEER web site, 2011.

[14] Okay, if you've never seen Chevy Chase in Fletch, this comment will make no sense. If you have, then you are probably laughing your butt off right now (pardon the pun). Just YouTube it…

Chapter 12

[15] Check out more of Bethany's story at bethanyhamilton.com or watch the movie "Soul Surfer".

[16] Loosely translated from Hebrew this means: "We praise you, O God, Healer of the Sick"

Chapter 14

[17] This prayer, more than any other, has changed my life. I encourage you to read it daily as you search for direction and answers in your journey. Send me an email, and I'll send you a beautiful desktop wallpaper with the prayer on it. The words come from "In Thoughts in Solitude, Part Two, Chapter II" and consists of 15 lines that have become known as "the Merton Prayer." See www.mertoninstitute.org for more great contemplative readings.

About the Author

ERIC W. SANDRAS, Ph.D.: With a degree in Human Development and Family Relations, has spent a decade as university and college professor and pastored churches for fifteen years. The author of three books: *Buck Naked Faith*, *Plastic Jesus*, and *Mystics, Mavericks, and Miracles Workers*, Eric continues to encourage countless people to seek God's grace in the "tough stuff" of life. Dr. E. lives in Colorado with his wife, Cindy, and two children, Carter and Dakota.

I have prayed for you ... that your faith may not fail"
(Luke 2:32).

Find Eric on the web at:
www.TheDailySteps.com
or follow him on Twitter: @ericsandras

Other Ampelon titles by Eric Sandras

Mystics, Mavericks & Miracle Workers:
A 30-Day Journey with Some Saints

Ancient writings of saints are often lost in today's world of self-help religious books. But for the saints who have traveled before us, they left a well-marked pathway to discovering a deep, authentic relationship with Jesus--one that reflects the way He lived and how He lived.

In this book, authors Eric Sandras and Jason Chatraw take a look at the writings of six saints (St. Francis of Assisi, St. Ambrose of Milan, St. John of the Cross, St. Teresa of Avila, St. Bernard of Clairvaux, and St. Catherine of Genoa) and show how their ancient words are still relevant to today's culture hundreds of years after they were first penned. They were mystics (people who sought to experience God daily), mavericks (people who bucked status quo), and miracle workers (people who experienced the supernatural power of God intersecting with the natural). From their well-worn path, we can learn much about faith and becoming the people God wants us to be.

Paperback, 160 pages
ISBN: 978-09786394-9-5
Also available in eBook format